ENGLISH FOLK SONG

ENGLISH
FOLK SONG

Some Conclusions

Cecil J. Sharp

Fourth (revised) Edition
prepared by
MAUD KARPELES
with an appreciation of Cecil Sharp by
RALPH VAUGHAN WILLIAMS

WADSWORTH PUBLISHING COMPANY, INC.

BELMONT, CALIFORNIA

Printed in Great Britain by
Bookprint Limited, Kingswood, Surrey

CONTENTS

Author's Note to First Edition

THE AUTHOR desires to express his grateful thanks to Dr R. VAUGHAN WILLIAMS, Dr W. A. SHAW and Mr HERBERT MACILWAINE for the interest that they have shown in the writing of this book, and for the most valuable criticisms and suggestions; to Mrs LEATHER, Miss LUCY BROADWOOD, the Rev. S. BARING GOULD, Mr FRANK KIDSON, Mr J. A. FULLER MAITLAND, Dr VAUGHAN WILLIAMS, Mr H.E.D. HAMMOND and Mr C. E. D. WARING for their courtesy in allowing him to quote tunes which they have collected and published in the *Folk-Song Society's Journal* and elsewhere; and to Messrs Novello and Co. Ltd, for giving him permission to include amongst the illustrations the Morris Tunes, 'Country Gardens' and 'Constant Billy'.   C. J. S.

Editor's Note to Fourth Edition

IN THE present edition a number of revisions have been made, mostly in the form of footnotes. Modifications of the original text have been indicated, with the exception of a few minor corrections and the omission of some redundant passages. The Editor's Preface is based on the one which appeared in the Third Edition of 1954, though it has been revised and brought up to date. The Bibliography (Appendix I) has also been brought up to date, and a new Appendix has been added containing the complete texts of eight songs together with four of their accompanying tunes which do not appear in the body of the book.

The editor acknowledges her thanks to Professor B. H. Bronson and to Mr Peter Crossley-Holland for valuable suggestions and advice which she received from them in the preparation of this present edition.   M. K.

CECIL SHARP

AN APPRECIATION

IT IS now just fifty years since Cecil Sharp startled England with *Folk Songs from Somerset*. We knew vaguely, already, that we had some traditional tunes in this country and that some of them, such as 'Dives and Lazarus' and 'My Bonnie Boy', were very beautiful. But such a wealth of beauty as this volume, containing, to mention only a few, 'High Germany', 'The False Bride', 'Searching for Lambs' and 'The Crystal Spring', was something we had never dreamed of. And where did it all come from? It was not a bit like Purcell or Arne or Bishop or Sterndale Bennett. Nor apparently could we trace it to watered-down reminiscences of Schubert or Mendelssohn. It must therefore be indigenous. But that was absurd. We knew, on the best authority, that folk music was 'all either bad or Irish'. But Sharp believed, and we believe, that there, in the fastnesses of rural England, was the well-spring of English music; tunes of classical beauty which vied with all the most beautiful melody in the world, and traceable to no source other than the minds of unlettered country men, who unknown to the squire and the parson were singing their own songs, and, as Hubert Parry says, 'liked what they made and made what they liked'. Of course there were strong men before Agamemnon, and there were collectors of folk song, in a small way, before Cecil Sharp. Indeed, if it had not been for these forerunners, Sharp could not even have started his great work. In the domain of theory, Parry had applied the Darwinian theory of evolution to music, and had proved the necessity of folk song. It remained for the big man to come along and combine theory and practice in one.

There was already a Folk-Song Society in existence which discussed our traditional melodies over a cup of tea in a dilettante spirit, and had to admit, rather shamefacedly, that some of these tunes sung by simple-minded rustics were 'sweetly pretty'. And in the domain of the ballad Allingham had suggested, tentatively, the idea of communal growth. Parry had theoretically traced the evolution of music from the primitive tune to the elaborate symphony. It was left to Sharp to declare, in no half-hearted manner, that here was something of supreme beauty which had grown up, as part of our life, with our language and our customs. And he set to work both by precept and practice to enable, at all events, the younger generation to recapture their great heritage of song which their fathers had nearly let slip through their fingers. The result was astonishing. Here were tunes obviously of the highest beauty which were nevertheless easy to understand and easy to sing. Sharp, who had no idea of hiding his light under a bushel, published several volumes of these wonderful tunes which the average amateur could easily sing, and fitted them with accompaniments which their sisters or girl friends could easily play. But Sharp's mind was set on the younger generation, and he insisted, after some trouble with the authorities, that folk song should be taught in school. So the battle was won and folk song is now a household word.

And how about the creative musician? Sharp in this book, *English Folk Song: Some Conclusions*, writes:

> Now . . . we have the musical ability, and we have the folk song: our first obvious duty is to see that the latter is restored to the nation as soon as may be . . . When every English child is, as a matter of course, made acquainted with the folk songs of his own country then, from whatever class the musician of the future may spring he will speak in the national musical idiom.

This prophecy has come true. It is not mere accident that the sudden emergence of vital invention among our English composers corresponds in time with this resuscitation of our own national melody. Of course there has been a reaction. The younger generation declare that folk songs had no influence on them. But much as they may dislike it, they can no more help being influenced by these melodies which have permeated the concert room, the school room, the stage and even the Church, than they can help speaking their own language. It is not something antique and quaint which Sharp has galvanized into a semblance of life. It is something which has persisted through the centuries, something which still appeals to us here and now and, if we allow it, will continue to develop through all the changes and chances of history.

February 1954   RALPH VAUGHAN WILLIAMS

EDITOR'S PREFACE

CECIL SHARP was born on 22 November 1859, and died on 23 June 1924.[1] He wrote *English Folk Song: Some Conclusions* in 1907, when he had been collecting for about four years and had noted some fifteen hundred tunes, mostly from Somerset. At his death he had noted nearly double that number in England and about 1700 in the Southern Appalachian Mountains of North America making a total of nearly 5,000.[2] In England his researches ultimately covered twenty-seven counties, including the County of London, but Somerset continued to be his main field of research. Since his death, no extensive collection of folk songs from England has been published, but our knowledge of folk song in the English language has been widened by Gavin Greig's collection of ballads from Aberdeen,[3] and also by the many collections of Anglo-American folk songs which have succeeded Cecil Sharp's pioneer work in the Southern Appalachians.[4] These have been gathered from many regions of North America: from the Maritime Provinces of Canada and Newfoundland as well as from the majority of the States.

The collecting of folk songs still continues both in England and America and interesting variants are from time to time being brought to light, but one may conclude that the corpus of extant English folk song has now been recovered. It is therefore possible to consider Cecil Sharp's views in relation to the field as a whole.

---

[1] For an account of his life, see *Cecil Sharp* by A. H. Fox Strangways and Maud Karpeles (Oxford University Press, 2nd Edition 1955).

[2] His manuscript collection is deposited in the library of Clare College, Cambridge.

[3] *Last Leaves of Traditional Ballads and Ballad Airs*, Gavin Greig, ed. Alexander Keith (The Buchan Club, Aberdeen, 1925).

[4] See *English Folk Songs from the Southern Appalachian Mountains*, Cecil Sharp, ed. Maud Karpeles, 2 vols. (Oxford University Press, 1932, 2nd impression 1952, reprinted 1962 in one volume.)

He did not himself regard his 'conclusions' as final (see pp. xx–xxi) and had he himself undertaken the revision of this book he would have wished to amplify certain passages in view of his wider experiences. For instance, the material that he discovered in the Appalachian Mountains would have induced him to enlarge on certain technical manifestations of folk song; to these we shall refer later. In the main, it can be said that his conclusions remain un-challenged even after a period of over fifty years, and one can only marvel at the insight and vision which enabled him to perceive the fundamental qualities and the true significance of folk song even with the comparatively limited material that was then at his dis-posal and the restricted area of his researches.

Since his death, and more particularly since the Second World War, research in folk music has proceeded apace in many countries. Yet Sharp's work has not been outdated: rather, it has in some ways gained in significance through being seen in the context of a wider field of studies. At the same time, this book, written when the collection and revival of English folk song were in their infancy, is of historic interest and offers a valuable comparison with the present scene.

The chapter on the Modes is perhaps the least satisfactory. Much of it is somewhat speculative and it should be read as depicting the background against which he worked rather than as an authorita-tive statement on the subject. We felt at liberty to re-write the section on the pentatonic scale (p. 65) since Cecil Sharp's later views were known to us, but we did not feel justified in revising the rest of the chapter, particularly as the historical aspect of the subject is still to some extent a debatable one. It is with the use of the modes in English folk music that we are mainly concerned, and here we are on firmer ground, for Cecil Sharp's statements on this aspect of the subject require but little modification.

Three dates stand out in the annals of Cecil Sharp's career as a collector of folk music: 1899, 1903 and 1916. At the end of 1899 he became aware of English folk music as a living art through the dancing of the traditional Morris 'side' at Headington, near Oxford; in 1903 he heard his first folk song, 'The Seeds of Love', from a traditional singer in the village of Hambridge, Somerset; and in 1916 he started on his voyage of discovery in the Southern Appalachian Mountains.

Writing in 1907, Cecil Sharp deplores the decline of folk song in England and states his belief that 'as recently as thirty or forty years ago, every country village was a nest of singing birds' (see p. 133) At that time he little thought that within a decade he would be experiencing conditions which, so far as folk song was concerned, approximated to those that would have obtained in an English village not thirty or forty but one or two hundred years ago. The scene of this happy anachronism was the mountain region of North Carolina, Tennessee, Kentucky and Virginia, where Cecil Sharp and the writer spent forty-six weeks during the years 1916 to 1918.[1]

The inhabitants of the mountains, who are of British descent (English, Lowland-Scots and Scots Irish) were at that time living in self-contained communities. Owing to lack of roads they had little contact with the outside world. They built their own log-cabins, grew their own food and made nearly all their clothing and utensils from the natural resources around them. They were mostly un-lettered and their music, like their fine manners, was not derived from instruction and training, but was an inherited tradition. With a few exceptions, their songs were the traditional songs that their forefathers had brought with them from the British Isles, and such changes as had been wrought during the course of time in the melodies and texts owed little or nothing to extraneous influences, but were the result of oral transmission working within the community.

Cecil Sharp's prophecy that 'in less than a decade English folk singing will be extinct' (p. 150) has happily not been borne out. Apart from the wealth of Anglo-American material, folk song is still to be found in England, although the situation both as regards quantity and quality has deteriorated since the days of which he was speaking. The writer recently made a selection from Cecil Sharp's notebooks of thirty-two Somerset singers who had had big or

[1] See *op. cit.*

valuable repertories and visited the villages, some dozen, in which they had lived, in order to find out whether any of their descendants or near relatives remembered the songs. The sons, daughters and grandchildren of eighteen of the singers were traced and enquiries were made from them and from many other people in the neighbourhood. The result was a total of six songs from three singers: a son, nephew and acquaintance, respectively, of Cecil Sharp's former singers.

Some years ago the writer made a similar experiment in the Appalachian Mountains and found that the decline in the singing of folk songs was very marked. This is not surprising, for the building of roads, the installation of electricity and the introduction of universal education have revolutionized the lives of the mountain people. The tradition is, however, even now more vital in the Southern Appalachian Mountains and in many other parts of North America than it is in England.

Cecil Sharp suggested that the belatedness of the harvest which twentieth-century folk-song collectors were gathering was not without its compensations, since the work was now being done accurately and scientifically, which was not the case with the collectors of a century or more ago (see pp. xix and xx). He did not, however, live to see the great advance that has been made in the recording of sound on magnetic tape, whereby present-day collectors are able to obtain an exact reproduction not only of the song but of its performance. In this way the minute deviations of pitch and rhythm and the delicate ornamentation, which make up the traditional performer's style of singing, and which often defy accurate notation, can be preserved for posterity. In this connection, one might amplify Cecil Sharp's remarks on ornamentation (see p. 32). Apart from the variations and passing notes he refers to, English folk singers will sometimes make use of subtly introduced grace-notes and slurs. These are perhaps intended not primarily as an embellishment of the tune, for one seldom hears a real trill or flourish, but rather as a means of giving emphasis and of maintaining continuity.

In America the mechanical recording of folk song has been

undertaken for many years by various learned institutions, notably the Washington Library of Congress. In England we have made a later start, but the B.B.C. has made laudable efforts towards salvaging the remains of folk song in the British Isles,[1] and this example has been followed by learned institutions such as the School of Scottish Studies, Edinburgh University. A critical survey of the material that has been recorded in the last decade has not yet been made, but it would seem that in England traditional survivals are not as scarce as one would have supposed, whilst in some parts of Scotland and Ireland the folk song tradition is even stronger than it is in England.

The decline in the traditional practice of folk song is not peculiar to England, but is to be found in most parts of the world: in fact, wherever primary education, industry and mechanical music have permeated. These and other factors of our modern civilization have all to a greater or less degree had a disruptive effect on the lives and outlook of those homogeneous communities which have in the past been dependent upon their own resources for their musical pursuits, i.e. the people whom we may, in fact, call the 'folk'. The immediate effect of their coming into contact with new ways of life is a tendency to reject many things which are associated with the past: folk song as well as other home-made products.

There is, however, some indication that this is merely a temporary attitude of mind, which springs from lack of self-confidence during a transitional period of adjustment. Many times singers who have dropped their songs, or their children who have never troubled to learn them, have regretted their negligence when they have realized that the songs were held in high esteem by others. And sometimes one is confronted with the ironic situation that a traditional singer, who has forgotten the words of his songs, will eagerly re-learn them from the printed pages which bear the record of the songs as he used to sing them years ago.

Oral transmission, which has been responsible not only for the

---

[1] The B.B.C. has presented a set of the folk-song recordings which it has made to the English Folk Dance and Song Society, and these may be heard at the Cecil Sharp House Library.

survival but for the gradual evolution of folk song, can now no longer operate freely as in the past. Once a song is written down, or once it is recorded, it emerges from its fluid state and becomes in a sense crystallized. It would seem therefore that the making of folk song, as we understand the term, is very largely a thing of the past. It belongs, as Cecil Sharp suggested (see p. 151), to a particular stage of human development. In fact, the history of folk song might be compared with that of language, in which the formative process is strongest in the period before it becomes a written language.

Though the making of folk song may belong to the past that does not mean that the article itself is outworn or valueless either to those who have inherited it by tradition or to those who have acquired it by conscious means. The permanent value of folk song, as Cecil Sharp has stressed over and over again, lies in its intrinsic artistic qualities, and it is by these that it must ultimately stand or fall.

During the nineteenth century, in spite of the literary interest in traditional ballads, English folk song as a musical expression was almost unknown to the educated classes of society and it carried on its unsuspected existence in the seclusion of our country villages. This ignorance of English folk song, which Cecil Sharp deplores in this book, has happily been remedied. This is due, in the first place, mainly to his own persistent efforts. For during the all-too-short period of twenty years which he devoted to English folk music (song and dance) he not only collected and published the material but spent himself untiringly in his efforts to bring it again into common currency. The result is that English folk song is no longer the exclusive possession of any one section of society, but it is known and loved, although still to a limited extent, by people in all walks of life.

Folk song is taught in the schools, it is to be found on gramophone records, it is a popular item in broadcast programmes. Thus we have the paradoxical situation that those very elements which helped to destroy folk song in the past are now among those that are contributing most effectively to its revival.

In the last chapter of this book Cecil Sharp discusses the future of

English folk song, and he conjures up a vision of the streets being flooded with folk tunes. The uncritical might be tempted to think that this happy circumstance had already come to pass, but the time is not yet, for only a small percentage of what passes as 'folk song' is the genuine article.

Cecil Sharp wrote his 'Conclusions' in order to dispel the erroneous conceptions which were commonly held at that time. The need to do so was all the more urgent since the educational authorities were recommending the teaching of folk songs in schools without any clear idea of what consituted a folk song. He believed that nothing would be more likely to prevent the eventual acceptance of folk song as common currency than the circulation of counterfeit or debased coinage. Now half a century later, it is more than ever necessary to stress that folk song and popular song are not one and the same thing. It is not the popularity of a tune that makes it a folk tune, nor does a 'composed' tune automatically become a folk tune merely by virtue of having been adopted by country singers and instrumentalists.

It is not easy, as Cecil Sharp recognized (p. 107), to coin a precise definition of the difference between folk and art music (or between folk and popular music). There are bound to be border-line cases, for folk music is part of the great world of music and there will always be mutual influences; but that is not to deny the hypothesis that folk music is a specific genre of music.

The International Folk Music Council, at a Conference held at São Paulo, Brazil, in 1954, adopted the following definition:

> Folk music is the product of a musical tradition that has been evolved through the process of oral transmission. The factors that shape the tradition are: (i) continuity which links the present with the past; (ii) variation which springs from the creative individual or the group; and (iii) selection by the community, which determines the form or forms in which the music survives.

To this definition, the following riders were added:

> (1) The term can be applied to music that has been evolved from rudimentary beginnings by a community uninfluenced by popular

and art music and it can likewise be applied to music which has originated with an individual composer and has subsequently been absorbed into the unwritten living tradition of a community.

(2) The term does not cover composed popular music that has been taken over ready-made by a community and remains unchanged, for it is the re-fashioning and re-creation of the music by the community that gives it its folk character.[1]

This definition, although it lacks precision, may be accepted as a guide to the fundamental concept of folk music. It coincides with the views held by Cecil Sharp, which he elaborates in Chapters 1 to 4, Chapter 9 (pp. 139ff) and Chapter 11.

We have already expressed the view that the further creation of folk songs in England is hardly possible, but that is not to say that musical creation is at a standstill. Songs will be created, whether they be popular songs or songs in the category of high art, but they will not be folk songs, although they may be influenced by folk song. Cecil Sharp believed that folk song would have a fertilizing effect on English music, and one cannot regard it as a mere coincidence that the twentieth century, which has seen the discovery of English folk song, has also seen a flowering of English musical composition such as has not been known since the days of Purcell. Some musicians have acknowledged this indebtedness to folk music. There are others who are speaking in a language enriched by the folk idiom who would nevertheless deny that folk music has been a source of inspiration to them. And this, perhaps, is as it should be, for (to quote Cecil Sharp) 'it shows that when some musician of genius has once demonstrated how the people's music may be translated into terms of art-music, the musical idiom of the nation is settled once for all and may be utilized and developed by composers, even when . . . they are themselves ignorant of their country's folk music'.

It would, however, be wrong to regard folk music merely as a foundation on which to build. Folk music is not embryonic music. It is complete in itself and should be judged on its own artistic

---

[1] *Journal of the International Folk Music Council*, VII, p. 23 (Cambridge, 1955).

merits. No one would claim that every folk song is a great work of art. That Cecil Sharp did not do so is shown by the fact that he published for general use only about ten per cent of the songs that he collected. But he did claim that the best of our English folk songs have that timeless quality which is the attribute of all great artistic creations.

MAUD KARPELES

September 1964

INTRODUCTION

THE SUBJECT of English folk song has recently been very prominently before the public. Twenty years ago, however, it was only by a very few people that folk songs were known to exist in this country; and even they, probably, were quite unprepared for the developments that have since taken place. At that time, and for several years afterwards, it was generally assumed that we had no folk songs of our own, and that the English peasant was the only one of his class in all Europe who was unable to express himself in terms of dance and song. How, in the face of facts as we now know them, such an amazing misconception could have originated, obtained credence, and escaped disproof for so many years, is an enigma which we will not here attempt to explain. It is enough that recent researches have finally disposed of the grotesque supposition. Those who realize all that this means, and who perceive the fresh prospects that have been brought into view, are naturally jubilant.

The question, too, admits of no doubt. Folk songs, genuinely and demonstrably English, have already been gathered in their hundreds, and of a quality at least as remarkable as their number. The work of collection, too, on any comprehensive scale, has only just begun. The larger part of rural England is still virgin soil; while of those districts that have already been visited, very few have, as yet, been explored with any degree of thoroughness. The future, therefore, may hold still greater surprises in store for us.

Nevertheless, a great movement has been initiated, public interest is aroused, and there is now little doubt but that this great and important national work will be prosecuted with vigour and earnestness, and brought to a satisfactory conclusion. True, it is a belated harvest that is being garnered. But even this is not without its compensations. For the work is now being done in the right spirit, scientifically, accurately, and above all with a scrupulous honesty and conscientiousness; and this is scarcely the way in which it would have been approached a century or more ago. The eighteenth-century musician had other notions, and was little disposed to trouble himself with any strict ethical considerations where the collecting and editing of the people's music were concerned. The present-day collector, however, sets up another and very different standard. He realizes that his first and chief obligation is to record just what he hears, no more and no less, and that the value of his work will depend upon the truthfulness and exactness of his transcriptions.

Manifestly, it would be premature at the present stage to essay a complete history of English folk song. An exhaustive treatise on the subject will some day have to be written, but for this we must wait until every scrap of the existing material has been recovered. In the meanwhile, those who are engaged upon the preliminary work of collection are gathering, day by day, songs and dance-tunes, and taking careful note of numberless minute but interesting and valuable facts that bear collaterally upon the subject of folk singing. Only those, perhaps, who have been brought into close contact with the old folk singers of today, can fully realize how intimately folk singing and folk dancing have, in the past, been bound up with the social life of the English village. It becomes, therefore, a matter of the highest importance that not only the songs, but that all things that relate to the art of folk singing, should be accurately recorded while there is yet the time and opportunity. They, one and all, form part and parcel of a great tradition that stretches back into the mists of the past in one long, unbroken chain, of which the last link is now, alas, being forged.

In the present volume I have recorded many of the characteristics of the folk singer, his manner of singing, peculiarities of intonation, his attitude towards tradition and so forth, all of which have come under my own observation. I have also enunciated certain theories concerning the origin and nature of the folk song, that have been deduced from these observations, and to which they seem to lead. Some of these, perhaps, in the fullness of time and in the light of wider research, may have to be modified. In the meanwhile, they are advanced, not in any dogmatic spirit, but cautiously and tentatively, in the hope that they may stimulate interest in the subject and, perhaps, attract the notice and kindly consideration of students and, in particular, of my fellow workers in other parts of England.

As I alone am responsible for the statements and theories contained in the following pages, the reader is entitled to know the nature and extent of those experiences of which they are the outcome.

It is eight years ago since I began, at first desultorily, to note down and collect English traditional music. During the last half of that period I have spent every available moment of my leisure in country lanes, fields and villages, in the quest of folk singers and folk dancers. Chance, in the first instance, guided my footsteps into Somerset, to which county my labours for the past four years have been almost exclusively confined. I have, so far, deliberately resisted the temptation to stray farther afield, because I believe that by concentrating my energies upon a limited area, instead of spreading them out over a wider one, I shall acquire information of especial value, and thus, perhaps, gain a deeper insight into the subject.

My collection contains, in round numbers, fifteen hundred tunes. Between twelve and thirteen hundred of these have been captured in Somerset, or, more accurately, in about two-thirds of that county, which is all that I have as yet thoroughly explored. These tunes consist mainly of song and ballad airs, the remainder being made up of sailors' chanteys, children's singing games, dance tunes, carols, and nursery rhymes. They have been noted down from upwards of 350 singers and instrumentalists.

With these statistics before him, the critic may object that the title *English Folk Song* is misleading, in that the book deals with the folk songs of Somerset rather than with those of England. This objection, however, is, I believe, more apparent than real. For, in the present state of knowledge, it is impossible to say how far the folk music that has survived in a county like Somerset is, or is not,

truly representative of English folk song as a whole. No authorita-
tive statement on this point can be made until every part of England
has been explored with equal thoroughness. In the meanwhile,
there is some warrant for the belief that the distribution of folk
songs throughout the kingdom is, to a large extent, independent of
locality.[1] This is the general conclusion at which I myself have
arrived after examining, and comparing with my own, the
material gathered by others, including the very large collection
made by the Rev. S. Baring-Gould in Devon and Cornwall. In this
view I have, moreover, the support of Dr G. B. Gardiner, who has
recovered a large number of songs in Hampshire. He says: 'I do
not believe that the public or even musicians are alive to the fact
that the songs we are collecting are the folk songs of England, and
that they are not confined to one county but are known throughout the length and breadth of the land.'

Be this as it may, I must confess that the conclusions contained in
the following pages are based for the most part upon the material
that I have myself collected, and the observations that have come
under my own notice.

Because of their familiarity, and for the sake of convenience, the
illustrations have, wherever possible, been culled from my own
note-books. Where they have been gathered from other sources
the names of the collectors are expressly stated.

The major portion of this volume is concerned with the music
only of the folk song. Rightly regarded, the two elements of the
folk song, the words and the melody, should be considered as
inseparable. They are so closely interwoven, one with the other,
that both suffer by dismemberment. This is especially true of the
words. The tunes, however, suffer far less by being presented alone.
In some cases, the omission of the text is an actual advantage, as, for
instance, with those old ballad airs that have been divorced from
their own proper words, and are, nowadays, allied to modern
verses of very small literary value.

In the past, moreover, far more attention has been paid to the
words than to the tunes of the old ballads. Most of the standard

[1] This has proved to be the case.

collections of traditional ballads give the words only. The collections edited by Herd and Buchan, for instance, contain no tunes at all; while those of Motherwell, Scott, Kinloch and Child include but a very small number. It is time, therefore, that the balance, as between the respective claims of the words and the tunes, should be restored. The folk tune presents many problems of absorbing interest to the musical theorist, and it is to the consideration of these that a large part of this book is directed. The theory of the evolutionary origin and growth of folk poetry has received its full share of attention during the last century or more; whereas, so far as I am aware, very little has been written upon the application of that theory to the folk tune.

It is, moreover, to the interest which the tunes, rather than the words, have excited, that the present folk song movement in England owes much of its impetus.

Nevertheless, I would deprecate any attempt to narrow down to a single issue the many questions which arise out of this most fascinating subject. Its many-sidedness is not the least of the many attractive qualities of the folk song. It spreads a wide net and entangles within its meshes specialists in many different branches of knowledge. The historian, musician, ethnologist, educationalist, social reformer, archaeologist and student of folk lore, are, one and all, attracted to its study. The field is a wide one, and there is plenty of room for workers in all these spheres of learning without jostlings or rivalries. If, therefore, in this volume the subject is treated more especially from the musical and educational points of view, this is not because in the opinion of the author these are the only, or even the most important of its many aspects, but simply because they happen to be those with which alone he feels himself at all competent to deal.

The main thesis of this book is the evolutionary origin of the folk song. Now, this is not a question of merely academic interest, but one upon which many practical considerations depend. The claims, for example, made by those who advocate the re-introduction of folk songs into our national life, all hinge upon this question of origin. They rest upon the assumption that folk music is generically distinct from 'composed' music; that the former is not the composition of the individual and, as such, limited in outlook and appeal, but a communal and racial product, the expression, in musical idiom, of aims and ideals that are primarily national in character. Once establish the fact that the folk song has not been made by the one but evolved by the many, and its national character and its fitness to serve a national purpose follow as a natural consequence. Musicians would then no longer place 'Tom Bowling' and 'The Seeds of Love' in the same category, but perceive that they typify, respectively, two distinct species of music, that differ not in degree but in kind. The educationalist, too, would be alert to the danger of confounding folk song with art song, and realize that, although both may serve his purpose, he must, nevertheless, be careful to assign to each a separate niche in the ideal educational scheme.

This point lay at the root of the controversy which recently took place over the action of the educational authorities with respect to the introduction of folk songs into the elementary school. Their action was adversely criticised, because it was based upon the misconception that the folk song proper and the 'merely popular song' were generically identical. To the outsider, and to those who are not expert in the subject, this, no doubt, seemed a matter of small moment, and the protagonists of the communal theory of the folk song were told that they were committing 'the common error amongst archaeological musicians of mixing up practical necessities with interesting investigations'. In point of fact, of course, they were doing nothing of the kind. They were enunciating a very important and fundamental principle, upon the clear understanding of which the whole question turned. Unfortunately, the subject was too large and of too subtle and complex a nature, adequately to be discussed in the columns of a newspaper.

The exposition of the communal theory contained in the earlier chapters of this book, will, it is hoped, put the matter in a clearer light, and enable the educational authorities to understand, even if they cannot agree with, the point of view taken by their critics.

For the last century and more the practice of singing folk songs has, in England, fallen into abeyance amongst all classes, save only the peasantry. A purifying and refining influence has thus, throughout this long period, been withdrawn from the nation, and not, I believe, without detriment to it. Now that English folk songs are being collected and published and brought within the reach of everyone, every effort should surely be made to popularize them once again amongst all classes of society. This book will have served, perhaps, its chief purpose if it aids, to however small a degree, the restoration of the English folk song to those to whom it belongs by right of inheritance.

LONDON, N.W.
August 1907.

CHAPTER I

DEFINITION

ALL FORMS of mental activity are due to the development and specialization of qualities that are natural and inborn. Education can create nothing; it can only develop those natural and instinctive faculties which already exist in rudimentary form. When these aptitudes are pronounced they will, under favourable conditions, reveal themselves without the aid of conscious or formal education, and will, in some cases, achieve results of a very remarkable kind. Indications, therefore, of those special gifts for which a nation is renowned will usually be conspicuous in the output of its lower and unlettered classes. The gift of epigram for instance, will be foreshadowed in the people's proverbs; the talent for literature and poetry in the tales and ballads of the common people; the spiritual and mystic sense in their myths and legends, and so forth.

If, therefore, we would gauge the musical potentialities of a nation we must look to the musical utterances of those of the community who are least affected by extraneous educational influences; that is, we must search for them amongst the native and aboriginal inhabitants of its remote country districts. Their own music, if they have any, will be the outcome of a purely natural instinct. If they have none, then we can be sure that the educated music of that country will be an artificial product, an alien importation, and comparatively worthless. A country that is too arid to grow wild flowers will scarcely win renown for the beauty of its gardens or for the excellence of its agricultural produce.

Now, as a matter of fact, in every land we do find music of a distinctive and often of a very beautiful quality, prevalent among the unlettered classes; bound, it is true, by certain limitations, but of a beauty and character of its own which colour although they may not be entirely shared by the educated or art music of the same nation. This spontaneous utterance is called *folk song*.

The word itself is a German compound, which of recent years has found a home in this country. Unhappily it is used in two senses. Scientific writers restrict its meaning to the song created by the un-lettered classes. Others, however, use it to denote not only the peasant songs, but all popular songs as well, irrespective of origin, *i.e.* in the wider and looser sense in which it is sometimes used in Germany. This is to destroy the value of a very useful expression, and to rob scientists of a word of great value. The expansion was, moreover, unnecessary. For the English language already possessed in the phrase 'popular song', a description which covered the wider field. There was, therefore, no need to do violence to the restricted and strictly scientific meaning of 'folk song' by stretching it beyond its natural signification. On the other hand there was a very good reason for coining a new term, or for importing a foreign one, to signify a peasant-made song, because our language contained no word with that precise meaning.

It is impossible to fix with certainty when the word folk song first became current in England, but it could not have been much more than twenty years ago. For it was in 1878 that Carl Engel contributed a series of articles to the *Musical Times* on the subject, which was afterwards issued in book form under the title *The Literature of National Music*. It is surely safe to assume that the author, himself of German extraction, would scarcely have used the expression 'national music' if the word 'folk song' had at the time been available. That Engel meant by 'national music' the music created by the peasantry is made plain in the following passage, in which he protests against the use of that expression in a wider significance:

> The great majority of the airs printed in Ritson's *English Songs* can evidently not be regarded as national airs in a strict sense of the term, although the tunes may have been for some time in popular favour. The same remark applies to the airs in almost all the English collections of old songs. The difference between a national song (German, *Volkslied*) and a merely popular song (German, *Volksthümliches Lied*)

is not always distinctly observed by the English musicians, and the two terms are often used indiscriminately.

Those, therefore, who claim the right to use the term folk song in the loose sense of popular song, are placing upon it a meaning never given to it by the scientific writers of Germany, the country of its origin.

The word folk song was added to the language when we had a use for it, and not before. Until quite recently it was popularly believed that we had no peasant songs in this country. It was not until after this superstition had been exploded that it became necessary to find a word to denote the songs of the peasantry, a term which would distinguish them from the 'merely popular songs'. This need led, no doubt, to the importation of the German expression. We can only deplore the ambiguity which has since become associated with the new word, for it has despoiled the language of a very useful term.

The word is, of course, not to be found in any of the older dictionaries; for some inexplicable reason it is omitted from the *New English Dictionary* (1901).[1] It is, however, included in the *Century Dictionary* (1889), where it is defined as follows:

A song of the people; a song based on a legendary or historical event, or some incident of common life, the words and generally the music of which have originated among the common people, and are extensively used by them.

The inclusion of the qualification 'generally' is unfortunate, for it vitiates what would otherwise have been an excellent definition. Funk and Wagnall's *Standard Dictionary* is more precise:

A song or ballad originating and current among the common people, and illustrating the common life with its interests and enthusiasms as derived from legend or story; also a lyric poem on a popular theme in the style of such a ballad.

[1] In the 1933 Supplement, folk song is described as a 'song originating from the people'.

The history of the kindred word 'folk lore' is an instructive one. It was first used by Mr Thoms in the *Athenaeum* in 1846. The Folk-Lore Society afterwards appropriated the word, and the question of its definition was debated at some length in the Society's Journal. Eventually Mr Gomme's definition was adopted, viz. 'The science which treats of the survivals of archaic belief and customs in modern ages.'

It is to be hoped that the Folk-Song Society will some day follow this excellent example and frame an equally clear definition of the term folk song. Theirs would be an authoritative pronouncement, which would restore to the word its scientific meaning, and provide those who are making a serious study of the subject with a word for which there is no synonym in the English language.

In this book the word *folk song* will be used exclusively to denote the song which has been created by the common people, in contradistinction to the song, popular or otherwise, which has been composed by the educated. We shall see later on that it might be possible to expand this definition by the addition of further qualifications, such as 'evolved', 'communal', and so forth; but for the present, it is enough for our purpose to define it as the song created by the common people.

The expression 'common people' is used in this definition, and elsewhere in this book, strictly in its scientific sense, to connote those whose mental development has been due not to any formal system of training or education, but solely to environment, communal association, and direct contact with the ups and downs of life. It is necessary that a sharp distinction should be drawn between the *un*-educated and the *non*-educated. The former are the half or partially educated, *i.e.* the illiterate. Whereas the non-educated, or 'the common people', are the unlettered, whose faculties have undergone no formal training, and who have never been brought into close enough contact with educated persons to be influenced by them.

In bygone days, the 'common people' formed no inconsiderable part of the population, and were fairly evenly distributed between urban and country districts. Nowadays, however, they form an exceedingly small class—if, indeed they can be called a class at all—and are to be found only in those country districts, which, by reason of their remoteness, have escaped the infection of modern ideas. They are the remnants of the peasantry, which originally consisted of those of the 'common people' who resided in the country and subsisted on the land. Consequently, at the present time the expressions 'peasant song', 'country song', and 'the song of the common people', all mean one and the same thing, viz. 'folk song', and may be used indifferently in contradistinction to the 'town song', or 'art song', *i.e.* the song of the cultivated musician. Strictly speaking, however, the real antithesis is not between the music of the town and that of the country, but between that which is the product of the spontaneous and intuitive exercise of untrained faculties, and that which is due to the conscious and intentional use of faculties which have been especially cultivated and developed for the purpose.

CHAPTER II

ORIGIN

THE DOMINANT feeling of mankind, civilized or uncivilized, is the desire for self-expression. It has been said that imagination rather than reason makes the primary difference between man and the brute. The animal lives in a world of present and immediate sensations, and is incapable of recalling past impressions, either for pleasure or for comparison. The mental life of the brute is thus a continuous series of disconnected sensations. But the mind of man, even of primitive man, is stored with pictures of his past experience, which he can reproduce at will. As, moreover, he derives pleasure from the exercise of this faculty of reminiscence, we find him, even in the savage state, dramatizing his adventures or reciting them in narrative form.

Mr Herbert MacIlwaine, who spent many years in the Australian bush, relates that he noticed one evening in camp a black boy chanting a song in monotone, the while he struck a log with rhythmic blows of his hands. On enquiry the aboriginal explained that he was narrating an incident that had occurred that day, when a spare horse had bolted and had been captured after an exciting chase.

Rhythm and metre are aids to memory. The Countess Evelyn Martinengo-Cesaresco records that a modern Greek folk singer once said to her, 'As I do not know how to read, I have made this story into a song so as not to forget it.' That is precisely what the Australian bushman was doing. The modern Greek and the antipodean native acted under the same impulse.

These incidents would seem to show that, historically, the folk song either preceded the folk tale, or was coincident with it. The latter is Mr Jacobs' view, expressed by him in his note to 'Childe Rowland', in his *English Fairy Tales*. He writes:

There seems to be a great probability that originally all folk tales of a serious character were interspersed with rhythm, and took therefore the form of the *cante-fable*. It is indeed unlikely that the ballad itself began as continuous verse, and the *cante-fable* is probably the protoplasm out of which both ballad and folk tale have been differentiated, the ballad by omitting the narrative prose the folk tale by expanding it.

The *cante-fable* consists of a prose story interspersed with verses which are sung or chanted by the reciter. Usually, as in Grimm's fairy tales, the verses occupy but a small space compared with the prose recitation. On one occasion, however, I noted down a version of 'Lord Thomas and Fair Eleanour', in which the whole of the story was sung, with the exception of three lines, which the singer assured me should be spoken (*F.S.J.* II, p. 108). This was clearly a case of a *cante-fable* that had very nearly, but not quite, passed into the form of a ballad, thus corroborating Mr Jacobs' theory.

The music contained in the *cante-fable* is always, of course, very rudimentary. Here is an example recorded by Mr Kidson (*F.S.J.* II, p. 295):

THE STORY OF ORANGE

Contrast this with the following example of savage music which Mr Herbert MacIlwaine heard chanted in chorus by Australian natives. The song is known as a 'corroboree', and is repeated over and over again throughout the ceremony of which it forms part. The native words are omitted.

AUSTRALIAN CORROBOREE

Numerous examples of aboriginal song have been recorded by travellers and others. In most cases the song of the savage is embedded in story, legend or ceremony, apart from which it has no separate existence; while its tune, like our Australian example, generally consists of a single strain, rambling and indefinite, which is repeated either at the same or at varying pitch. Such tunes record the earliest attempts of primitive man to express himself through the medium of music and, as such, are of profound interest. They are at the best, however, very rudimentary, and their kinship with modern music is exceedingly remote. Folk song proper belongs to a later stage of development. The dividing line should, perhaps, as Sir Hubert Parry suggests in his *Art of Music*, be drawn between music that consists of a single phrase, and that in which two or more phrases are employed. Of the two examples quoted above, the first is the less elemental, because it contains two different strains of melody, which are contrasted, thereby showing some rudimentary feeling for design. The Australian song, on the other hand, has but one amorphous phrase which is repeated as often as the performer wishes. Although the gulf which separates the formless song of the savage from the patterned tune of civilized man is a very wide one —there may be geological ages between them—the former is, nevertheless, the prototype of the latter.

Whatever theory of the origin of the folk song be accepted, it is not difficult to realize the causes which, in the main, have led to its genesis. But we are faced with a problem of far deeper complexity when we come to trace the course of its descent. Before, however, we embark upon this investigation there is a preliminary objection which must be discussed.

In the preceding chapter we have defined the folk song as 'the song *created* by the common people'. This definition involves the assumption that the folk song is the unaided composition of the unskilled; and this few, perhaps, will be prepared to concede offhand. To some it will seem fantastic to credit the unlettered peasant with the capacity to compose music, good, bad, or in-different. For, by general admission, the technical difficulties with which the musician has to contend are at least as great as those which confront the sculptor or the painter; yet one may search in vain in the country village for evidences of the peasant image or picture-maker. Surely, it will be argued, it is far more probable that the folk song is only the fashionable song of a bygone day, the composition of the skilled musician, which found its way into the country villages where, although long ago forgotten in the town or city of its origin, it has since been preserved. To put it in another way, the folk song, it is contended, is not a genuine wild-flower, but, in the jargon of the botanist, a 'garden-escape'.

On the face of it, this looks the easier and more plausible explanation; and it evades a very awkward assumption. But, unfortunately, it does not square with facts. For, if the music of the common people originated in the towns, the sheet music and song books of the past would surely bear evidence of the fact. And this they fail to do. To search for the originals of folk songs amongst the printed music of olden days is mere waste of time. Moreover, there is a further difficulty. Composed music differs generically from folk music; it belongs to a different order. Folk music, as we shall presently see, is distinguished by certain technical peculiarities, which are absent from art music; while, on the other hand, art music possesses many musical attributes which are not to be found in the music of the common people, or in that part of it which we call folk music. But, apart from technical differences, the extreme naturalness, the spontaneity, freshness and unconventionality of folk music are just those qualities which are conspicuously absent from the popular-song music of past centuries. Indeed, folk music is as distinct from art music as is the wild flower of nature from the gorgeous blooms of the cultivated garden. As well search for a wild rose in a well-kept garden, as for a folk song in the song books of the past.

These considerations force us to the conclusion that folk music has in some way or other originated amongst those who play and sing it; that it is the product of the folk muse, and that neither the skilled musician nor his compositions have inspired its creation. How this has come about is another matter, which must now occupy our attention.

On this question experts are divided. Some hold that folk songs were composed by individuals just like other songs, and that they have been handed down to us, more or less *in*correctly, by oral tradition. Others, however, maintain that folk songs are the products not of the individual, but of a people or community, and that we are indebted to the process of oral tradition, not only for preserving them, but for creating them as well.

This question of origin formed the subject of a long and acrid controversy on the Continent during the first half of the last century. The brothers Grimm were the leading protagonists of the communal theory, which was hotly attacked by Schlegel and others; while some straddled the fence and ascribed the origin of the folk ballad partly to individual and partly to communal effort.

It is true that the dispute centred round the words of the folk song rather than its music; but this does not affect the question at issue. For it is clear that the life history of the music of the folk song has been, in principle, the same as that of the words.

The Grimms held that folk poetry 'makes itself'; that 'epic poetry is not produced by particular and recognized poets, but rather springs up and spreads a long time among the people themselves, in the mouth of the people'; that folk poetry was slowly and unconsciously evolved in the same way as language. 'How does a race make its language?' they asked. 'In mass or by deputy?'

This was a very pretty theory and, on the face of it, sounded plausible enough. But the Grimms supported it by assertion rather than by argument. They did not condescend to explain the precise manner in which poetry 'made itself' ; or the exact way in which the 'communal mind' bridged the gulf between inspiration and concrete expression. This was the weak spot in their case and their opponents were not slow to seize upon it.

Schlegel, for example, ridiculed in caustic language the vagueness of their utterances. 'A poem,' he maintained, 'implies a poet; just as behind every work of art there sits the artist. Legend, ballad, and proverb might be the property of the people, but they were nevertheless the work of the individual, not of the community. A crowd of workmen, no doubt, carry the stones and beams and do the actual building of the cathedral; but they act under the direction of the architect, and his are the ideas which they translate into terms of bricks and mortar. With such scornful scoffings did Schlegel meet the vague assertion that 'the song sings itself'.

Uhland took up a midway position between these extremists. On the one hand he conceded that 'in poetry of the people there is a decided preponderance of the mass over the individual'; 'but,' he added, 'this poetry can get utterance only through individuals.' So at one moment he agreed with the Grimm theory, only in the next to uphold the individualistic theory of Schlegel.

In Scotland, Motherwell favoured the communal view. In the introduction to his *Minstrelsy*, he talks vaguely and indefinitely— after the manner of the Grimms—of the 'Universal Mind', and of its 'intellectual and moral tendencies'. But he does not enlighten us as to what he means by this 'Universal Mind', nor how, in practice, it works and expresses itself in terms of words and music.

On the other hand, Bishop Percy and Sir Walter Scott ascribed the origin of the ballad to the individual work of the trained minstrel, 'professing the joint arts of poetry and music', or, maybe, to 'the occasional effusions of some self-taught bard'.

Boehme, like Uhland, alternately faces both ways. He tells for instance, in his *Altdeutsches Liederbuch*, of a certain leprous monk of the fourteenth century, who lived on the banks of the Rhine and made songs which the people loved and sang, scattering them all over the land. 'There,' says he triumphantly, 'we have the secret about the origins of popular poetry; the oft-admired and nebulous composition by a poetic multitude is mistake and nonsense. First of all one man sings a song, and then others sing it after him, changing what they do not like.'

Nevertheless, later on in the same book, he swallows these words, and asks: Why enquire for the author of a folk song when it was never really composed at all? 'It is a masterless and nameless affair.'

These are, of course, no more than the main features of a controversy, which originated, perhaps, with F. A. Wolf's attack on the Homeric poems (1795), and which wandered into numberless by-paths, down which it is not necessary for us to adventure. If the reader would pursue the subject he should consult the writings of the controversialists themselves. Or we would refer him to an admirable essay upon the subject—to which we are largely indebted for the above abstract—by Mr F. B. Gummere, in the introduction to his *Old English Ballads* (Ginn and Co., Boston, U.S.A.).[1]

And now, where lies the truth of the matter? We would suggest that it is to be found in the writings of the disputants on both sides. It is best expressed, perhaps, in the words of Boehme, already quoted; 'First of all one man sings a song, and then others sing it after him, *changing what they do not like.*' The italicized words contain the kernel of the nut. The solution of the mystery of the origin of the folk song is to be found not by seeking for an original —that is a vain quest—but by examining the method by which it has been preserved and handed down from one generation to another. In other words, the method of oral transmission is not merely one by which the folk song lives; it is a process by which it grows and by which it is created.

The folk song must have had a beginning, and that beginning

---

[1] A useful summary is also given in C. Brouwer's *Das Volkslied in Deutschland, Frankreich und Holland* (The Hague, 1930).

must have been the work of an individual. Common sense compels us to assume this much. Otherwise we should have to predicate a communal utterance that was at once simultaneous and unanimous; and that assumption even Jacob Grimm would have hesitated to make. Whether or not the individual in question can be called the author is another matter altogether. Probably not, because the continual habit of 'changing what they do not like' must, in the course of time, ultimately amount to the transference of the authorship from the individual to the community. The following illustration will, perhaps, explain this point.

Let us suppose that an individual, A, invents a story and tells it to his friend, B. B, if the story takes hold of him, will narrate it to C, but in doing so will consciously or unconsciously—it matters not which—make some changes in the tale. He will very likely locate it in his own neighbourhood, change the names of the *dramatis personæ* to those of his own friends and relatives, and in countless small ways 'improve' upon the tale as he received it from A. C in passing on the story to D, will, in like manner, add to it his own 'improvements'. D, E, F, etc., will follow the same example. The story will thus leave each individual of the series in a different form from that in which it came to him. By the time it reaches Z we may, without doing violence to probability, conceive that the story has become so changed that it bears no longer any resemblance to the form in which it originally left the mouth of A.

Who is the author of the story which Y tells to Z? Certainly not Y, because he had it from X; nor X, because it came to him through W; nor V, U, T, etc., for similar reasons. Nor, finally, can A be credited with its invention. Indeed, he would not himself claim it; for, by our hypothesis, his original tale has been so changed during its passage from B to Z, that he would not even recognize it, much less claim its authorship. The author has disappeared. The most that can be said is that the authorship belongs equally to all those who have taken part in the transmission. Thus, the authorship, originally individual, has become communal. The individual has vanished, and the community has slipped into his shoes.

For simplicity's sake we have assumed that A related his story to one friend only. But in all probability he would tell it to many others as well. Instead, therefore, of one B, there will be many B's. Now each of the latter will in turn relate the story, with personal variations of course, to his own circle of friends; so that the number of C's will be very much larger than the number of B's. As, therefore, we proceed down the series represented by the letters of the alphabet, the number of those concerned in the transmission of the story will increase at every step; increase, too, by geometrical progression. So that, by the time that Z is reached, the number of persons in possession of the narrative will be enormous. And, be it remembered, no two of these individuals will be relating their stories in exactly the same form.

Manifestly, this is the process to which all things preserved by oral tradition have necessarily been subjected. All products of the primitive mind that are preserved orally and are not written down are in a perpetual state of flux. The very conditions of their existence postulate change and growth. This is in accord with the experiences of the collector of traditional tales, legends, proverbs, dances or songs. Each time that he notes down a particular tale or song he will record it in a different form. The collector of folk songs, for instance, knows that it is only very rarely that two singers will be found to sing the same song in precisely the same form.

These several forms are not corruptions in varying degree of one original. They are the changes which, in the mass, engender growth and development. They are the suggestions of individuals, akin to 'sports' in animal and flower life, which will only be perpetuated if they win the approval of the community. Nor are these different forms necessarily or widely distinct from each other. On the contrary, when the collector comes to compare his variants of a particular song, he will usually find that they will readily submit to some simple scheme of classification, and that he can easily place each of them into one or other of quite a small number of categories.

Moreover, although the variations are very numerous they will not all be preserved. Manifestly, those alterations will alone survive which commend themselves to other singers and narrators and are imitated by them. Consequently, the folk tale or song, throughout its life-history, will always be approaching a form which will accurately express the taste and feeling of the community; what is purely personal will be gradually but surely eliminated.

How these communal characteristics become impressed upon the traditional tale or song may be demonstrated if—to revert to our original illustration—we assume that *A*, an Englishman, tells his story to *b*, a Frenchman, who circulates the tale amongst his own countrymen. The additions and changes that the successive narrators will now introduce into *A*'s story will obviously be very different from those which were made in the former case. The Frenchman is less downright and practical-minded than the Englishman; he is more fanciful, but less imaginative; his sense of humour, too, if less exuberant, is more subtle than that of the Anglo-Saxon. Manifestly, the story would sooner or later be coloured by these national traits, and, ultimately, the two versions, narrated respectively by *Z* and *z*, would differ very materially from one another; differ, indeed, just as the character of the Englishman differs from that of the Frenchman.

This is not idle speculation. It is possible to confirm it by an appeal to fact. For there are many ballads, which, alike in subject, have been current traditionally in different parts of Europe. In all such cases the treatment accorded them by different nationalities varies very considerably. Let the reader, for example, compare the Scottish form of the words of 'The Two Magicians' (Buchan's *Ancient Ballads*, i. p. 24), or the Somerset variant (*F.S.F.S.* I, No. 19),[1] with the versions of the ballad as it is sung in the South of France (Child's *English and Scottish Popular Ballads*, No. 44). Here he will see three very different settings of one and the same story, the treatment in each case bearing the impress of racial characteristics. Many other and similar examples are to be found in the late Professor Child's admirable collection of ballads above referred to.

The themes of some folk ballads may, originally, have been

[1] Also *Selected Edition*, II, p. 8 and *English Folk Songs for Schools*, p. 10.

drawn from fact. Where, however, the fact has not been recorded in any written or printed document, the tale or ballad has proceeded along its evolutionary path unhindered. The original incident has passed from the memories of the narrators and there is no chronicled version to control their imaginations. This may even happen for a while in the case of a legend respecting a popular hero, whose doings are, nevertheless, recorded in written history. In such a case the historian eventually steps in, produces documentary evidence, proves the falsity of the story and stays its evolution. The well-known saying, 'Up, guards and at them!', attributed to Wellington, is possibly an instance of this.

Printed songs or instrumental compositions show a similar tendency in the hands of those who habitually play or sing them from memory. These alterations can never, of course, stray very far, for there is always the text to refer to, and the critic to call attention to it and to restrain the performer. Nevertheless, in some cases, where an individual variation has won general approval, it has come, in the process of time, to be accepted as a traditional 'reading'. The point to be remembered is that, as a general rule, evolution can only take place in song or tale for any length of time in the absence of an authoritative original.

The process of communal composition above described is not fundamentally different from the method of every individual creative artist. One is only a magnified reproduction of the other, on an immense scale; in principle they are identical. A melody is not suddenly born in the composer's mind ready made, complete in every detail. On the contrary, it assumes many shapes, and suffers innumerable changes before it reaches the form which satisfies him and which he ultimately uses. When these preliminary processes take place entirely within the mind of the composer, we can only speculate as to their extent and character. Mozart, for instance, is said to have arrived at the musical expression of his ideas with great speed, and without putting his hand to paper until the process of composition was completed.

But with Beethoven it was otherwise; he not only laboured long and painfully in the act of composition, but, happily for us, recorded in books each idea as it occurred to him. As many of his pocket-books have been preserved, it is possible to trace the successive stages through which some of his most celebrated melodies passed, from the germinal forms in which they first came to mind, down to the final states with which we are familiar. In some cases the melody in its ultimate form bears so little resemblance to the original draft, that, without a knowledge of the intervening links, it would be difficult to believe that one had been evolved out of the other—just as difficult, indeed, as it was to connect Z's tale with A's original form of it.

Now the successive forms through which a melody passes in the mind of a composer during the process of composition correspond to the variants of a folk song. Both sequences represent successive attempts to consummate the expression of some ideal, consciously or unconsciously preconceived; in both cases they record the stages in a process of evolution. That process, it is true, is controlled, in one case, by an individual, in the other, by a community. This will affect the course of the evolution, and the musical character of the finished product; but the method is, notwithstanding, precisely the same in each case.

Those critics, therefore, who argue that folk song variants are corruptions of some mysterious original, must, if they would be logical, regard the first draft of a Beethoven melody as the original, and all subsequent developments as corruptions, including, of course, the melody in its final and published state.

In both individual and communal compositions it is comparatively easy to trace the course of development when once the evolutionary process has been brought into action. The actual beginning of the folk song, however, presents greater difficulties. We have already argued that it is impossible to resist the assumption that every traditional song, tale, or legend began with an individual invention of some sort. But we have also seen that, in the course of its descent through the ages, the folk song undergoes ceaseless and continuous change. Consequently, given the time, it will inevitably and ultimately assume a shape that bears little or no similarity to the form which it bore at its inception. The initial form, therefore, cannot properly be regarded as the original or prototype of the folk song in its later states, to which it bears no resemblance. It is, rather, the source from which it sprang, the starting-point of its subsequent career.

With respect to the nature and character of the folk tune in its primary state there is not much to be said. There is, however, some evidence bearing upon the point.

Probably every collector has occasionally noted down folk songs which the singers have claimed to be their own compositions. Usually the claim covers the words only, but sometimes it includes the tune as well. The tunes on these occasions are usually of little value, consisting in the main of a string of the best known and most commonly used folk tune phrases. An exception to this generalization may, perhaps, be seen in a tune, in the mixolydian mode, which Miss Lucy Broadwood recently noted down in Ireland from Miss Bridget Geary, and which, together with the circumstances under which it was recovered, are recorded in the *Folk-Song Journal* (III, pp. 37–8). But this, I think, can scarcely be regarded as a typical example; it is, rather, the exception that proves the rule.

Sometimes singers will sing through a long ballad to a rambling and indefinite tune. On one occasion, for instance, a Somerset singer recited to me the words of a Robin Hood ballad. When asked to sing it, he at first demurred, but after some pressure consented to do so—'just as I sing it when I'm a-milking'. I soon saw it was quite impossible to note down the tune. The singer sang well, and after the manner of the regular folk singer. He kept, moreover, to one key and to one mode—the mixolydian. His phrases, too, were all interesting and rhythmical, and they fitted the words of the ballad accurately enough. But the tune as a whole was indefinite; it varied with every verse and wandered from phrase to phrase after the manner of a very free improvisation. A Gloucestershire singer gave me a similar experience. He sang in much the same fashion as the Somerset singer, except that his song was 'The Golden Vanity', and his tune was in the dorian mode.

It is conceivable that a tune sung in this rambling, go-as-you-please method, might, in course of time, and in the mouths of other singers, gradually become stereotyped into the form of a definite and patterned tune, which would thereafter be subjected to the evolutionary process in the usual way. The minstrels, no doubt, often improvised their words, but this habit did not prevent their ballads from ultimately assuming more or less a definite shape; and the same may be predicated with respect to the tunes.

We may, perhaps, assume that every folk tune began in one or other of the two methods above described. Very probably the more recent song tunes began in the first of these two ways, that is as defined and regularly formed melodies, made up of well-known phrases; while the older ballad airs originated in the second way, as vague and indefinite improvisations. This, of course, is mere speculation. In the nature of things there can be no absolute proof. The folk song is, therefore communal in two senses; communal in authorship, and communal in that it reflects the mind of the community. That, no doubt is what Motherwell meant when he said that the people's ballad was 'the actual embodiment of their Universal Mind, and of its intellectual and moral tendencies'. And the Grimms, too, were on the right track. Where, however, actual demonstration was imperative, they took shelter behind poetic phrases which, although they embodied much that was true, were singularly unconvincing. The demonstration that we have given is an attempt to supply what they failed to give, and to reach by logical steps conclusions which, if not identical with theirs, are very nearly so.

We have seen, then, that communal authorship and communal expression are the natural corollaries of oral transmission. This conclusion is of the utmost importance, for it allows us, even at this early stage, to draw a distinction between folk music and art music.

Art music, then, is the work of the individual, and expresses his own personal ideals and aspirations; it is composed in, comparatively speaking, a short period of time, and, by being committed to paper, it is for ever fixed in one unalterable form

Folk music, on the other hand, is the product of a race, and reflects feelings and tastes that are communal rather than personal; it is always in solution; its creation is never completed; while, at every moment of its history, it exists not in one form but in many.

CHAPTER III

EVOLUTION

IN THE preceding chapter it was shown that the essential features of the folk song, as we know it, may or may not have belonged to it at its inception. Many, perhaps all of its most characteristic qualities, have subsequently been acquired during its journey down the ages, and represent the achievements of many generations of singers. Individual angles and irregularities have been gradually rubbed off and smoothed away by communal effort, just as the pebble on the sea-shore is rounded and polished by the action of the waves. The suggestions, unconsciously made by the individual singer, have at every stage of the evolution of the folk song been tested and weighed by the community, and accepted or rejected by their verdict.[1] The life history of the folk song has, therefore, been not only one of steady growth and development; there has also been a tendency always to approximate to a form, which shall be at once congenial to the taste of the community, and expressive of its feelings, aspirations, and ideals. It is clearly a case of evolution.

Now the conception of evolution involves the three principles of *continuity*, *variation*, and *selection*. Let us take these three principles, one by one, and examine them.

CONTINUITY

Insistence of type must be the rule, and variation the exception. Otherwise, types would be so quickly changed and multiplied that their relationships one to another would be obscured, their genealogies concealed, and order give place to chaos.

To those unacquainted with the mental qualities of the folk, the

---

[1] This verdict is not to be interpreted as a conscious concerted appraisal of innovations by the community, but as the sum-total of the acceptance or rejection of such innovations by the individual members of the community.

process of oral transmission would be accounted a very inaccurate one. The schoolman, for example, accustomed to handle and put his trust in manuscripts and printed documents, would look with the deepest suspicion upon evidence that rested upon the memories of unlettered persons. In this, however, he would be mistaken, as all collectors of folk products know well enough. My own experience enables me to vouch for the amazing accuracy of the memories of folk singers. Here are two examples.

Not long ago I noted a song from Mrs Harriet Young at West Chinnock in Somerset. She told me that she had learned the song from some mummers who performed in her village about thirty years ago. She had never heard it sung since then, and she could only remember one verse of the words. A few weeks later, I noted down the same ballad from Mrs Susan Williams of Haselbury-Plucknett. Mrs Williams told me the same story; that she had heard it sung by the mummers who visited her village about thirty years ago—evidently the same troupe that had performed at West Chinnock. She also gave me but one verse, but the tune to which she sung it was, note for note, identical with that which I had noted from Mrs Young. I have never heard the air sung by anyone except these two singers, and they were strangers to one another.

Again, a blind man, one Mr Henry Larcombe, also from Haselbury-Plucknett, sang me a Robin Hood ballad (see p. 28). The words consisted of eleven verses. These proved to be almost word for word the same as the corresponding stanzas of a much longer black-letter broadside preserved in the Bodleian Library.

The words of the ballad have since been reproduced in other books, e.g., in Evans' Old Ballads, but, so far as I am aware, they have never been printed on a 'ballet' or stall copy, or in any form that could conceivably have reached the country singers. I cannot but conclude, therefore, that Mr Larcombe's version, accurate as it was, had been preserved solely by oral tradition for upwards of two hundred years.

It would be easy to multiply instances of this kind without going beyond my own experience; but these are sufficient for our purpose. The accuracy of the oral record is a fact, though, I admit, a very astonishing one. Less astonishing, perhaps, when we remember that the memories of the unlettered are, for obvious reasons, far more retentive and trustworthy than those of cultivated people. The traditional singer, moreover, regards it as a matter of honour to pass on the tradition as nearly as possible as he received it. When I have asked a singer, as I have constantly had to, whether he sang a particular song, I have often received the reply: 'No, I have heard it, but do not sing it; it is so-and-so's song.' On these occasions it is useless to press the singer; 'I have never learned the song and could not sing it exactly right', will be his honourable plea.

Such experiences as I have just related may tempt the collector to attach an exaggerated value to the accuracy and trustworthiness of the traditional record. Edward Bunting, for instance, in the preface to his *Ancient Music of Ireland* (1840), goes so far as to state that, although the words of the popular songs vary according to the several provinces and districts in which they are sung, 'yet the case is totally different with the music'. 'A strain of music,' he says, 'once impressed on the popular ear, never varies.' This statement asserts too much. Singers vary their tunes as well as their words—at any rate according to my experience. That they do this also in Ireland, anyone can see who will take the trouble to examine the *Petrie Collection of Ancient Irish Music*. Nevertheless, the fact that so eminent a collector as Edward Bunting allowed himself to be betrayed into such a statement shows how deeply he had been impressed by the accuracy of oral tradition.

It will be noted, however, that Bunting threw doubts upon the trustworthiness of the oral record where words, as distinguished from music, were concerned. This is not in accordance with my own experience, as I have already shown, nor, I may add, with that of other collectors. Motherwell, for instance, has an interesting passage bearing upon this point in the introduction to his *Minstrelsy*.

He says:

But fragile and capricious as the tenure may seem by which it has held its existence for centuries, it is worthy of remark how excellently well tradition serves as a substitute for more efficient and less mutable channels of communicating the things of past ages to posterity. In proof of this, it is only necessary to instance the well-known ballad of 'Edom o' Gordon', which is traditionally preserved in Scotland, and of which there is fortunately extant a copy in an English MS., apparently coeval with the date of the subject of the ballad. The title of this copy is 'Captain Care'. . . . Between the text of the traditionary version and that of the MS., a slight inspection will satisfy us that the variations are neither numerous nor very important. . . . Could, however, there be MS. copies of other of our ancient ballads recovered, it certainly would be a most desirable acquisition. If any such exist, and shall at any time hereafter be communicated to the world, it is confidently anticipated that they will establish the fact of tradition being in all matters relative to popular poetry, a safe and almost unerring guide. . . . It is not therefore with the unlettered and the rude, that the oral song suffers vital and irremediable wrong. What they have received from their forefathers, they transmit in the same shape to their children.

VARIATION

Before we discuss the causes which lead to variation, attention must be drawn to one extremely important characteristic of the folk singer. It is a well-known fact that the folk singer attaches far more importance to the words of his song than to its tune; that, while he is conscious of the words that he is singing, he is more or less unconscious of the melody. I have come across many peasant singers who were unable to recognize a tune, or at any rate to distinguish one tune from another. The following experience is a very common one and illustrates the point. It is a good plan, when you are striving to overcome the nervousness of a new singer, to ask him whether he sings some well-known ballad, such as 'The Unquiet Grave'. He will probably say that he does, and this admission will give you the opportunity of singing to him a verse or two of your own version of the ballad, and of asking him whether that is the way in which he is wont to sing it. He will very likely agree that it is. Later on, when you are on better terms with him, and he is no longer nervous, you will ask him to sing a verse or two of 'The Unquiet Grave'. In nine cases out of ten his version will prove to be quite different from that which you just now sang to him, and which he had assured you was the same as his. This is so frequent an experience that I have been driven to seek for some general explanation. The only one that I can offer is that when a peasant sings a song, or listens to one, his attention is exclusively occupied with the words, and he is quite unconscious of the tune. Had you tripped in your words, when in the first instance you sang to him, he would have corrected you at once. Not so, however, with regard to the tune, as we have seen.

I do not infer, because the singer is not thinking of the melody of his song, that the tune, therefore, conveys no pleasure to him. On the contrary, I know that it does. But his appreciation is sub-conscious rather than conscious. Some singers are, of course, more tune conscious than others, but I have never met with a singer who could detect small melodic differences. So long as your tune is, in the main, similar to his, the most musical of folk singers will declare it to be identical, although the differences may be of considerable importance from a musician's point of view, e.g., a change of mode, or a variation in rhythm.

I once heard a man sing 'Brennan on the Moor' in a village inn the rest of the company taking part in the chorus. They all agreed with regard to the words of the refrain, but many of them sang different versions of the air, no one, as far as I could see, making any attempt to adapt his own particular version to that of his neighbour. I believe that they were one and all quite oblivious of the cacophony they were producing, which grew worse rather than better as the song proceeded.

The inability, too, of the average English singer to hum an air without its words provides further proof of the peculiarity under discussion. Last Christmas, I was noting a song from a woman whose memory failed her at the last two lines of the first verse. I was not anxious to have the words, for I had taken them down on a previous occasion from another singer, but the tune was a fine one and a new one to me, and I wished to secure it. I pressed her, there-fore, to hum the last strain without the words. After some hesitation she complied, and I noted down the music. Just before I left her cottage she said she thought she would be able to recall the missing lines if she went out and walked in her garden for a while. On her return she sang the whole stanza without hesitation and, as I was quite prepared to find, the music of the last two lines proved to be quite different from that which she had previously hummed to me.

A similar experience is recorded by Miss Lucy Broadwood in the *Folk-Song Journal* (II, p. 198). Miss Broadwood relates that she once persuaded a singer to hum the tune of a song to her which he had refused to sing with its words, as they were 'outway rude'. He at once 'got confused, saying that he never could sing without words. His rhythm was impossible to note.'

This, however, is the tune as Miss Broadwood noted it down (*F.S.J.* I, p. 150).

SALISBURY PLAIN

First version

Some years later, the same singer sang the ballad in question, with its words, to Dr Vaughan Williams, who tells me that the tune was almost identical with that which he had previously noted down from another singer and which he has recorded in the *Folk-Song Journal* (II, p. 196):

SALISBURY PLAIN

Second version

Again, singers will often sing the first verse of a song to the whole tune, and then for the remaining verses repeat over and over again the second half only of the melody. Whenever this has happened to me I have questioned the singer and tried to discover whether or no he was conscious of his maltreatment of the tune. I have always come to the conclusion that he was not.

I am not in a position to say how far this inability on the part of the English peasant to sing a tune without its words is shared by the folk singers of other nations. M. Bourgault-Ducoudray, however, mentions the existence of the same peculiarity amongst the peasants of Brittany, and quotes a Breton proverb, 'Celui qui perd ses mots, perd son air.'[1]

Fiddlers, too, associate the tune with the dance in precisely the same way as singers connect the air of a song with its words. I have often heard them say that if only they could recall the dance they would remember the tune also. They seem quite incapable of playing a tune if they have forgotten the form and figures of the dance to which it belongs. On one occasion, a concertina player from whom I had just noted down a Morris tune innocently

---

[1] The singers of the Appalachian Mountains appeared to be more tune-conscious than the English traditional singers, for they were often able to hum or whistle a tune without its accompanying words. Gavin Greig had similar experiences in Aberdeenshire (*Last Leaves,* p. xiii).

remarked: 'Now, sir, you know all about the dance.' On cross-examination, I discovered that he really believed that a knowledge of the tune carried with it the knowledge of the figures of the dance also.

Now, this face has an important bearing upon the question of variation. For, manifestly, if the singer is habitually unconscious of the tune that he is singing, any variation that he may introduce will be unconscious and unpremeditated also. Causes can sometimes be suggested which may account for variation, but, in most cases, melodic alterations apparently spring spontaneously from out the heart of the singer. Mr Henry Larcombe, the blind singer whom I have already introduced to the reader, is a case in point. He will habitually vary every phrase of his tune in the course of a ballad. I remember that in the first song that he sang to me he varied the first phrase of the second verse. I asked him to repeat the verse that I

ROBIN HOOD AND THE TANNER[1]

---

[1] *Selected Edition*, I, p. 8.

[2] In Cecil Sharp's day it was usual to employ the key-signature of the minor (or major) scale of the relevant tonic and to make the necessary adjustments in the tune by means of accidentals. This method has been retained throughout the book.

might note the variation. He at once gave me a third form of the same phrase. I soon learned that it was best not to interrupt him, but to keep him singing the same song over and over again, in some cases for nearly an hour at a time—the patience of these old singers is inexhaustible. In this way I have been able to catch and note down those variations, which have recurred two or three times, but, of course, I have missed many of those which have appeared but once. I give below two of his tunes with, in each case, the variations that I noted down from him. They will repay careful study.

LORD BATEMAN[1]

First Version

<hr />

[1] *Selected Edition*, I, p. 17 and *Folk Songs for Schools* No. 1262.

The phrase-variations of these two tunes are very ingenious, and many of them are of great beauty. They display inventiveness of a high order, as well as a wonderful feeling for the modes. Such a singer as Mr Henry Larcombe is, of course, very exceptional; in my experience he is unique.

Important variations of this order are generally stereotyped and limited to a certain fixed number in each tune. In such cases they are probably less individual, and cannot all be credited to the invention of the singer. In 'Bruton Town', for instance, sung to me by Mrs Overd of Langport, the final phrase appeared in four different forms. These variations were not, however, attached to particular verses, although Mrs Overd never sang the ballad to me without introducing all four of them.

BRUTON TOWN

Singers like Mrs Overd and Mr Henry Larcombe belong to those who aid very materially the evolution of the folk song. The variations of the ordinary singer are comparatively trivial, as we shall presently see. But those given in the above examples are more than mere changes of detail; they amount to the invention of new phrases. Probably every generation has produced a small percentage of singers like Mr Larcombe or Mrs Overd, and to their especial gifts must be attributed many of those musical qualities which are the glory of the folk song.

Nothing less than inspired invention can have gone to the making of the types of variation which we have been just considering. Ordinarily, however, it is quite possible to suggest reasons which have led to melodic alterations. For instance, variations will often proceed from the love of ornament. Wherever in the course of a melody there occurs a long sustained note, the singer will be under the temptation to vary the monotony by the introduction of turns, trills, or passing notes. The extent to which singers will embellish their tunes varies with particular individuals and with the

peoples of different nationalities. In Scotland and Ireland folk
singers are especially given to this habit, and they will often bury
their tunes under a profusion of ornament (see *F.S.J.* III, pp. 3–38).
The Hungarian gypsies, too, are renowned for their love of
decoration. But the English singer uses ornamental devices more
sparingly. He prefers his tunes unadorned, and, if he occasionally
introduces notes of his own, they are generally passing notes,
designed to bridge a leap in the melody, or to provide notes for
extra syllables in particular verses. I give below some interesting
variations which were sung to me by a Bridgwater singer. They
are clearly individual changes, and I believe they arose from his love
of ornament.

ERIN'S LOVELY HOME

Another frequent cause of variation arises when the singer,
having partially forgotten his words, has substituted corrupt and

unmetrical lines. The attempt to adapt the tune to these irregularities will often lead to the invention, unconscious of course, of
interesting melodic changes. 'The Trees they do grow high', sung
to me by Mr Harry Richards of Curry Rivel, is an instance of this.

THE TREES THEY DO GROW HIGH[1]

In each stanza the tune of the first eight bars was sung as in
stanza I.[2]

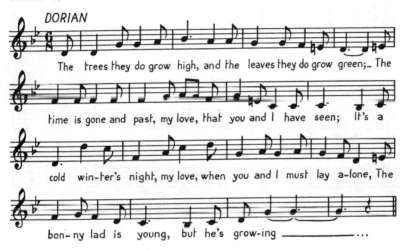

Second stanza

---

[1] Selected Edition, II, p. 20.
[2] The complete set of words is given in Appendix II, p. 892.

Third stanza

I will buy you a bunch of white rib-bons to tie a-bout his bon-ny, bon-ny waist, __ To let the la-dies know that he's mar-ried. _____

Fourth stanza

At the age of eigh-teen, my love, O his grief was grow-ing grief, And so she put __ to an end to his grow-ing. _____

Fifth and sixth stanzas

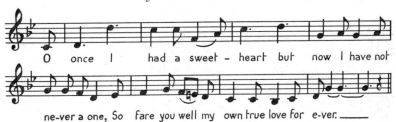

O once I had a sweet-heart but now I have not ne-ver a one, So fare you well my own true love for e-ver. _____

Yet another source of variation springs from the attempt to adapt an old tune to new words of slightly different metre. Singers will sometimes learn new sets of words from a ballad sheet, and, being ignorant of the proper tune, will sing them to an air with which they are familiar. If, as must frequently happen, the metre of the words is not exactly the same as that of the tune, they will alter and adapt the latter to meet the new conditions. I believe this to be a very fruitful source of variation. Even when metrical difficulties are absent, aesthetic considerations may lead to variation. For any emotional incongruity between words and tune will, sooner or later, be insensibly felt by the singer, and eventually lead to melodic variation in the attempt to bring words and tune into closer aesthetic relationship.

Change of mode is another cause of variation. Singers often display an individual preference for one particular mode. I have known singers nearly all of whose songs are cast in the dorian mode; others who evidently have an especial liking for the mixolydian mode, and so on. Now, change of mode generally means change of melody. Musicians know that it is only occasionally that a major tune can be converted into a minor one, or vice versa, without material alteration. Each mode has its own characteristic idioms, and its peculiar cadences. Consequently, change of mode is of the nature of free translation rather than of exact transposition. As an instance of this I will cite the well known folk tune 'Come all ye faithful Christians'. On the next page will be found versions of this air in the major, minor, dorian, mixolydian, and aeolian modes.

COME ALL YE FAITHFUL CHRISTIANS

From the Rev. S. Baring Gould's MS. Collection

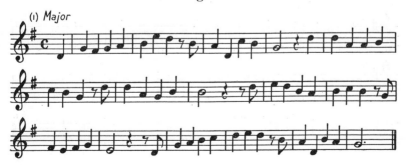

(1) Major

From Chappell's Popular Music

(2) *Minor*

(3) **DORIAN**

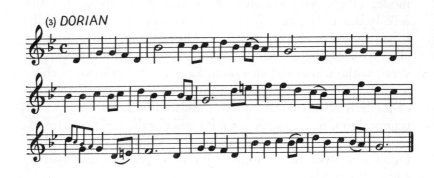

(4) **MIXOLYDIAN**

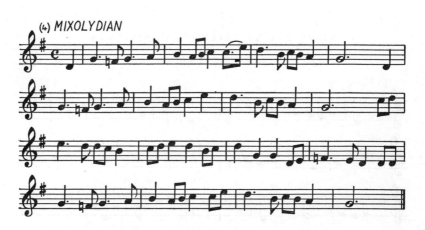

Noted by Dr R. Vaughan Williams

(5) AEOLIAN

The second of these is the tune of the well-known song 'The Miller of the Dee'. As it stands, it is not, I think, a folk-utterance. It has evidently suffered at the hands of the unscrupulous, and provides an excellent example of the hybrid folk tune, the 'Old English air', which has so often passed for the genuine folk tune, and which is still claimed as such by the uncritical. That the tune was, probably, an aeolian air when it first came into the hands of the musical editor, is, to some extent, proved by the last of the following examples, which was sung to Dr Vaughan Williams to the same words, 'The Miller of the Dee'.

There are, of course, many other causes of variation besides those already mentioned. I have confined myself to those that have come within my own personal experience. Mr Allingham, in the introduction to his *Ballad Book*, enumerates some of these. Talking of ballad words that have been preserved by oral transmission, he says:

> Passing from mouth to mouth and generation to generation of singers and reciters, dull and clever, undergoing numerous alterations by the way by reason of slips of memory, personal tastes, local adaptations and prejudices, additions, omissions, patches, and lucky thoughts, and, on the whole, gaining in strength in the process . . .

It must be borne in mind, too, that any change, however small, may eventually lead to results out of all proportion to the initial variation—just as an extra feather in a bird's tail has led to the evolution of the fan-tail pigeon.

SELECTION

In the evolution of species of the animal and vegetable worlds, those variations will be preserved which are of advantage to their possessors in the competition for existence. In the evolution of folk tunes, as we have already seen, the corresponding principle of selection is the taste of the community. Those tune variations which appeal to the community will be perpetuated, as against those which attract the individual only. The nature of that appeal may be of two kinds. It may be an appeal to the sense of beauty, *i.e.* aesthetic in character; or it may be an appeal to the understanding, *i.e.* expressive in character. Which of these will be the determining factor in selection will depend, ultimately, upon the racial characteristics of the community. The Celt, will, in all probability, be attracted by those variations which are primarily sensuous, and which satisfy his somewhat ornate feeling for beauty; whilst in the case of the Anglo-Saxon those variations which make for self-expression will be given the preference.

The tunes that I have recovered in West Somerset, where the people, to judge by their speech, are partly Celtic, are certainly smoother and more polished than those that I have gathered in East and Mid-Somerset. A rugged and forceful tune, like 'Bruton Town', seems to me to typify the Anglo-Saxon, one in whom the need of self-expression is the dominant feeling.

But this, I admit, is highly speculative; it would be wiser, perhaps, to wait until a larger amount of material is available before forming conclusions. Nevertheless, it is evident that the musical taste of every community must vary, and, as that taste is the controlling factor in the evolution of the folk song, national peculiarities must ultimately determine the specific characteristics of the folk songs of the different nations.

Having now considered in turn the three principles of *Continuity*,

Variation and *Selection*, we are in a position to ascribe to each the part it plays in the drama of the evolution of the folk song.

Without the first, *Continuity*, no evolution can take place. Its function is to prepare the way. It is a passive rather than an active agent; a condition, not a cause.

The second principle, *Variation*, creates the material which renders development possible. Variation, of itself, does not necessarily lead to development. Change may produce growth, or it may be sterile; or, again, it may lead to corruption.

The function of the third principle, *Selection*, is to ensure that variation shall, in certain cases, result in organic growth and development. Of itself, variation merely provides the building material, the bricks and mortar. The moulding of that material, the business of construction, the determination of the form that the building shall take, these are the work of *Selection*.

Moreover, *Variation* is the product of the individual; whereas *Selection* is the act of the community. The folk song, therefore, has derived its communal and racial character solely through the action of the third principle, *Selection*.

The illustration, given in the last chapter, demonstrated how changes, introduced by the individual, may, under favourable conditions, lead to development. It left, however, the manner of that development to be inferred. In the illustration which follows, this point will be exhibited more clearly.

There are few things in nature more wonderful and more incomprehensible than the ordered flight of a flock of starlings. Many thousands of these birds will fly together in a compact mass; they will wheel about in the air and describe orderly evolutions, without hesitancy, and with a precision which argues complete unanimity of purpose. If attention be concentrated upon the bounding lines of the moving and living mass, it will be noticed that these are not so clearly defined as, when casually observed, they appear to be. The edges, instead of being smooth and even, are rough and jagged. Further observation will show that these irregularities are due to the aberrations of flight on the part of individual birds, who are constantly separating themselves from their fellows, darting out at acute angles to the line of flight, and then swiftly returning to the flock. Every now and again, however, it will be seen that one of these birds is followed by all the rest, and the course of flight of the whole mass is immediately changed.

It is here that we must look for the explanations of those varied evolutions which at first seemed so puzzling. The erratic movements of the birds on the margin are so many invitations to the flock to change the direction of its flight. Ordinarily, these invitations are ignored; the flock prefers to remain on its course and will not be tempted to change it. When, however, one of these suggestions happens to coincide at the moment with the will of the majority, the invitation is accepted; the flock changes its course and a new evolution is initiated.

The same principle guides the action of every crowd of human beings, in the absence of an acknowledged leader. Suggestions are constantly being made to it by its members, and when, as must happen sooner or later, one of these receives general approval, it is automatically accepted, and the crowd acts as one man.

These two illustrations are, I believe, faithful pictures of the way in which a folk song is evolved. Of the innumerable changes made by individual singers, only those that win general approval are perpetuated; the rest, being ignored, pass into oblivion.

The causes which lead to variation have no material significance. They may or may not be relevant to the issue. The starling, for instance, may have left the ranks with the express purpose of luring the flock in its direction; but, more probably, its action was due to something else, to mere waywardness or to the search for food.

In like manner, the changes which singers introduce into the words or melodies of their songs proceed from many causes forgetfulness, chance, accident and what not; but very rarely, if ever, from a definite and conscious desire to improve.

The individual, then, invents; the community selects. It is necessary to dwell upon this point because it is one which is often misapprehended by the opponents of the communal theory. Only the other day, for instance, in reviewing a book of traditional ballads, the critic quoted a couplet from 'Sir Patrick Spens', scoffed at the possibility of its communal origin, and exclaimed that such lines as those could only have sprung from the brain of an individual. Of course they did. Every line, every word of the ballad sprang in the first instance from the head of some individual, reciter, minstrel, or peasant; just as every note, every phrase of a folk tune proceeded originally from the mouth of a solitary singer. Corporate action has originated nothing and can originate nothing. Communal composition is unthinkable. The community plays a part, it is true, but it is at a later stage, after and not before the individual has done his work and manufactured the material. Its part is then to weigh, sift, and select from the mass of individual suggestions those which most accurately express the popular taste and the popular ideal; to reject the rest; and then, when more variations are produced, to repeat the process once more, and again once more. The process goes on unceasingly while the ballad lives; or until it gets into print when, of course, its process is checked, so far as educated singers are concerned.

The racial character of a ballad or song is due, therefore, not to communal invention, but to communal choice. The form in which 'Sir Patrick Spens' has come down to us is stamped in its every line and every word with the hall-mark of communal approbation. The lines which the reviewer quoted may have reached us unaltered, in the exact form in which some individual first conceived them; or, as is far more probable, they have, since then, passed many times through the crucible of popular criticism. It matters not which. In either event, as they now stand, they reflect the popular taste, express the popular ideal, and are stamped with the popular approval. Communal action means just this and no more.

CHAPTER IV

CONSCIOUS AND UNCONSCIOUS MUSIC

IN THE preceding chapter we have seen that folk music, being
un-written music, lives only in the minds and memories of
those who sing it; that it is in a constant state of growth, each
singer unconsciously contributing something of his own to every
song that he sings; that these minute alterations are imitated or
ignored by other singers according as they appeal to them or not;
that folk music is thus, at every stage of its evolution, being
continually moulded into conformity with the taste of the community; that it is, therefore, communal music, not individual; and
that, proceeding from out the heart and soul of a nation, it em-
bodies those feelings and ideas which are shared in common by the
race which has fashioned it.

The genesis of music was the same as that of language in that
both were born in response to the human cry for self-expression.
The primitive singer did not reflect upon the notes that he sang;
he gave no thought to their exact pitch, nor to the order in which
he sang them, any more than the primitive word-maker reasoned
about the nature of the grunts which originally did duty for words.
He sang or talked because it pleased him, and because it satisfied
some inward feeling which called for expression.

His first musical efforts were of necessity very simple and rudimentary, amounting, perhaps, to no more than a monotone varied
by an occasional and arbitrary inflection of note. The second stage
was reached when a few sounds, connected by simply related
intervals, were strung together and formed a musical sentence or
phrase of sufficient individuality to fasten upon the memory. This
formula would be repeated over and over again, aimlessly and
without purpose.

A further advance was made when two of these phrases, having
nothing in common, were sung alternately. This could only be

accounted an improvement upon the single phrase because of its increased complexity. As a vehicle of expression, there was not much to choose between the repetition of a single phrase and the arbitrary alternation of two.

The fourth and final stage was attained when two or more phrases, involving the principles of contrast and repetition, were so combined as to form an intelligible pattern; a whole as distinct from its parts.

The single phrase is no more than the material out of which tunes are made. The simplest melody, in its modern sense, requires for its construction at least two phrases, just as the shortest piece of poetry must contain not less than two lines. As we have already pointed out, it is a far cry from the single-phrase music of the savage to the patterned melody of civilized man. A tune, as we understand it, is an organized structure, made up of proportioned parts, which are arranged according to some intelligible law of succession, and involve the elements of contrast and repetition, the whole conveying to the mind a definite impression.

When this stage of development had been reached, music had become an efficient instrument of expression, and men soon became conscious of it as something that had a separate existence of its own, altogether apart from the purpose that it served. They then proceeded to examine it, to analyse its structure, and to deduce therefrom laws and syntax. This marked a new epoch. What had hitherto grown up unconsciously and at the call of instinct was henceforth to be manipulated consciously, and developed by reasoned intention. The advent of the grammarian heralded the birth of art music.

The new order did not, however, extinguish the old. The people went on making and singing their own songs, unaffected by the growth of art music amongst the cultivated. Thus, we find, even at the present day, the two streams of art music and folk music flowing side by side. In the country, where nowadays the un-lettered classes alone survive, the common people still preserve their own music, just as they have kept their own speech. The history of music and of language has been very much the same.

Literature has been built upon the speech of the common people, as art music has been founded upon their music. Peasant music is genuine music; peasant speech is genuine language; neither peasant music nor peasant speech is a corrupt form of the music or of the speech of cultivated people.

The uncritical often overlook this. They confound the common language of the illiterate with the dialect of the unlettered, and refuse to distinguish between the instinctive music of the common people and the debased street music of the vulgar. They think that because folk music has been evolved without conscious reference to rule and principle, that it must on that account be second-rate music, of necessity inferior to the music composed by the educated musician. This, of course, is not so. Very often, indeed, it is all the other way. For the unconscious output of the human mind, whatever else it may be, is always real and sincere. A man, in his involuntary actions and unconsidered utterances, must, of necessity, expose his real nature; whereas those things which he does and says of set intention may or may not be sincere, and may or may not, therefore, reflect his true character.

The music of the common people must always, therefore, be genuine and true; for instinct is their only guide and the desire of self-expression their only motive. With art music this is not always so. The art musician practises his art of intention. He has expended time and thought upon his training, He is a specialist, and music is his trade. Consequently, he is tempted, when the inspiration is not upon him, to make music for the sake of making it, to turn it out mechanically, to use his head and not his heart, to divorce feeling from expression. The folk musician, on the other hand, working unconsciously and guided alone by the light of nature, is under no such temptation. He practises his art only when feeling and the desire of expression compel his utterance.

Now, these are just the conditions under which true art is brought to birth. We should, therefore, expect to find, as indeed we do find, that the unconscious music of the folk has all the marks of fine art; that it is wholly free from the taint of manufacture, the canker of artificiality; that it is transparently pure and truthful, simple and direct in its utterance. And these are the invariable attributes of the people's music. Folk melodies may not always appeal to us with irresistible force, or strike us as transcendently beautiful; but they are always sincere, and free from that pretence and affectation which are the invariable concomitants of bad art in general, and of bad music in particular.

Folk music, then, just because it is unconsciously produced, is in its essence good music. It is also scientific music. That is to say, it is constructed on well-defined, intelligible principles. Folk music is the ungarbled and ingenuous expression of the human mind, and on that account it must reflect the essential and basic qualities of the human mind. Language came before grammar, and music before the sciences of harmony and counterpoint were thought of. The laws of grammar are not the inventions of the grammarian. His business is faithfully to record what is common usage and to systematize the results of his enquiries. Music and literature are correct or incorrect just as they conform or not to the practice of writers and musicians of recognized repute. The grammarian simply tells us what that practice is. The fundamental laws and principles of music, that are nowadays known to every skilled musician and are consciously used by him in the exercise of his craft, were first enunciated in the music of the common people. A French writer has expressed this truth very aptly:

We must not be astonished if we come across myths which surprise us by their ingenious direction, or even by their profound philosophy. This is often the character of the human mind. . . . The human mind when it works thus spontaneously is a philosopher, just as the bee is a mathematician.

A comparative analysis of the mythological beliefs and super-stitions of the several nations of the world goes to prove that the minds of men at equal levels of cultivation are everywhere sub-stantially the same; what is due to the particular race is the particular development of the belief or superstition. And this is undoubtedly true of folk music. For, although folk tunes of different nations differ from one another, and they all differ in certain respects from art melodies, yet they are one and all constructed upon the same fundamental and scientific principles.

CHAPTER V

THE MODES[1]

THE SCALES upon which many English folk tunes are constructed are not the same as those with which we are familiar in classical music. They are sometimes known as the Greek modes[2] and they certainly figure very prominently in Greek literature. But the Greek writers, of course, did not invent them; they merely explained them. Presumably, it was from the folk that they derived the material which they analysed, and from which they deduced their theories. The Greeks were the earliest musical grammarians in Europe, and they laid the foundations of a scientific system, of which, in a modified form, we are the inheritors, both in our folk song and in plain-song.

The subject of this chapter is, of course, only indirectly related to that of folk song. The fact, however, that a large number of our folk tunes are cast in the modes has awakened a new interest in these ancient scales. Hitherto, that interest has been confined to the church musician, or to the antiquarian and to him of an academic cast of mind; and in such hands the practical musician has been content to leave them. For it has been customary to look upon the ancient modes as mere relics of a bygone day, archaic scales, which were employed in the early days of art music in default of something better, but which were eventually discarded in favour of a system better suited to modern requirements.

But the recent discoveries of English folk song have thrown a fresh flood of light upon the matter, and have attracted the attention and interest of many of the younger and more enterprising musical spirits of the day. For here are scores of melodies, cast in the old

[1] Bertrand H. Bronson's article on 'Folksong and the Modes' (*Musical Quarterly*, xxxii, No. 1, January 1946, pp. 37–49) can with advantage be read in conjunction with this and the next chapter. The reader is also referred to the article on 'Modes, Musical' by Peter Crossley-Holland in the *Encyclopaedia Britannica* (1965 edition). See also Preface, p. x.

[2] Nowadays they are more often known as mediaeval modes.

modes, yet throbbing with the pulse of life, beautiful, attractive, expressive, and making, withal, a powerful appeal to modern taste and feeling. Manifestly, such melodies as these cannot be quietly dismissed as archaic survivals, and relegated, as such, to the lumber room. Old they may be, measured by years, but there is a modernity about them, vivid and unmistakable, which proves that they are also young, and that the spring of youth is still in them. Nor, again, are they to be confounded with the music of the church. Except for the fact that they happen to be cast in the same scales, they have but little in common with the melodies of plain-song.[1]

Clearly they represent a type of melody which breaks fresh ground, and offers a wider horizon, and new possibilities to the modern composer. That the latter is keenly alive to these possibilities recent events have abundantly shown. For these reasons it has been thought advisable to include in this book a chapter dealing with the modes.

As to the technical explanation of this difficult subject, the briefest summary must suffice.

The white notes of the pianoforte form a *diatonic scale*, which may be defined as *a series of sounds arranged in alternate groups of two and three tones respectively, each group being separated from the next by the interval of a semitone.*

Each octave of the diatonic scale is thus spanned by seven steps, five of which are steps of a tone, and two of a semitone. The seven notes in each of these octaves are called natural notes and are named after the first seven letters of the alphabet.

When the notes of the diatonic scale are referred to one principal and fundamental note—called the *tonic*—the resulting scale becomes a *mode*. As each one of seven natural notes, a—g, may be used as a tonic, the number of modes is seven, as follows:

DORIAN

---

[1] More recent writers see a connection between the melodies of folk song and plain-song.

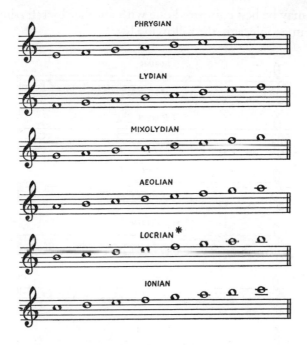

The Greek names by which the scales in the above list are distinguished, are not attributed in accordance with ancient practice, but as they are familiarly known to English musicians.

These seven modes are all diatonic, because each consists of a series of alternate groups of two and three tones, separated by semitones. The relationships which the several notes of each mode bear to their tonic depend upon the order in which the intervals follow one another; and this varies with each mode. For instance, the semitones in the dorian mode fall between the 2nd and 3rd notes, and between the 6th and 7th; in the phrygian the semitones fall between the 1st and 2nd notes, and the 5th and 6th, and so on. Thus, each one of the seven modes has its particular sequence of intervals, peculiar to itself, by which it may be recognized, and from which, moreover, it derives its distinctive character. The

* See last paragraph of page 55.

modes may be best compared one with another by referring them
to the same tonic, as in the following list:

The principle of *tonality* or *modality* lies in the predominance of
the tonic as the ruling note of the scale, and as forming the link
which connects all the notes of a composition. When this predominance is asserted throughout a given melody, then and then
only is the mode clearly defined, and its individuality impressed
upon the character of the music.

It is a moot point whether or not the ancient Greeks ever
acquired a sense of tonality according to the above definition of that
term. Many authorities believe that in the time of Aristoxenus
(c. 350 B.C.), the so-called modes were no more than segments of
one mode, in which case we can only conclude that the Greeks of

that period possessed but a rudimentary sense of mode. It would, undoubtedly, be difficult to cite a single passage from the writings of Aristoxenus to prove that the scales which he propounded were regarded by him as separate and distinct modes. But, at the same time, it must be borne in mind that our knowledge of his musical system is very imperfect, for it is based upon those portions only of the three Aristoxenean treatises which have been preserved. Be this as it may, there is evidence which goes to prove that, in post-classical times, the Greeks did acquire a sense of modality comparable with that possessed by modern musicians. The writings of Ptolemy, for instance, seem to indicate that in his time, *i.e.*, 150 A.D., the use of the different modes, or specific forms of the diatonic octave, had become general. Although it may not be possible to establish this by direct quotation from the works of Ptolemy himself, or from those of his contemporaries, there are many passages which are difficult to interpret on any other supposition.

Now, it is stated by Helmholtz that in the time of S. Ambrose (340–397 A.D.), the rule was enunciated that every melody should end upon its *final*, or, as we should say, the *tonic* of its mode. This rule would, of course, signify an understanding of the meaning and of the importance of tonality. Very soon, however, according to Helmholtz, exceptions to this rule began to creep in. Under certain circumstances, a melody was allowed to end upon other notes, called *confinal tones*, as well as upon the final. This led to dire confusion, and, despite the formulation of fresh rules, it became increasingly difficult to determine the mode to which a given melody belonged. Eventually, certain fixed concluding phrases, or 'endings', became associated with each mode, and it was by these only that the mode could be recognized. The introduction of this artificial and mechanical method of determining the mode marked a serious decline in the sense of modality.

It should be mentioned that Helmholtz gives no authority for his statement with respect to the Ambrosian rule, which cannot, therefore, be accepted without reservation. It derives some support, however, from the fact that two centuries later a system of scales was propounded, which, from the point of view of tonality, was

far less satisfactory than the Ambrosian. This system was introduced either by Pope Gregory himself (c. 540–c. 604), or during
his life-time. The Gregorian system included a new form of scale or
so-called mode, designed to differentiate between melodies which
were in one and the same mode, but which differed in compass.
Church musicians would distinguish, and still do so, between the
modes in which, for instance, 'Greenland Fishery' and 'Lord
Rendal' are cast, simply because the former melody lies between
the dominant and its octave, and the latter between the tonic and
its octave.

GREENLAND FISHERY[1]

LORD RENDAL[2]

To the modern musician, it seems superfluous to distinguish
between the scales in which these melodies happen to lie; for the
compass of a melody is a quality which he regards as accidental

[1] *Folk Songs for Schools*, No. 963 (Set. 2).
[2] *English Folk-Songs for Schools*, p. 4.

and not essential.[1] To him the essential quality of a melody is derived from the relationships which its several notes bear to their tonic; and these relationships are altogether independent of the compass of the melody. But, in the early days of musical history, with the Greeks as well as with the Church, and before the real nature of the mode was apprehended, this was not understood. It seemed quite natural, for instance, to the player of an instrument of limited compass, to distinguish between those tunes which he could or could not play upon his instrument. It may be that it was this difficulty which confronted Aristoxenus, and led him to distinguish by name the several octaves of his one mode—if this is what he really did. Whether the Greeks of a later day ultimately solved the problem or not, it is difficult to say. But it is certain that no real progress could be made in the science of music, until the theorists had learned to differentiate between 'accidental' and 'essential' scales—to borrow terms used by Helmholtz.

The Greeks, it should be remembered, made the tetrachord—the scale of four notes—the unit of their scale, not the octave; and they expended an immense amount of time and ingenuity in devising methods by which the tetrachords might be combined, and the compass of the scale extended. As a method of scale analysis, this was radically unsound and led nowhither.

The common habit of picturing the scale as a succession of ascending or descending notes is one that leads to much confusion of thought. The essential feature of a scale is the relationship which each of its component parts bears to the tonic. The order of the intervals which these successive degrees make is a matter of secondary importance. It is to this habit of viewing a scale as a succession of conjunct sounds that much of the misapprehension which exists with regard to the modes must be attributed. For the modes, when they are set out in the usual way (see pp. 48–49), look very much alike. Seeing this similarity and noticing, moreover, that they are all constructed out of the same seven sounds, the

[1] According to Professor Bronson 'the range has a significant relation to the shape of the tune, and cannot be safely ignored in comparative analysis' (*The Traditional Tunes of the Child Ballads*, I, p. xxviii). See also his article, 'Folk-Song and the Modes' in *Musical Quarterly*, xxxii (1946), pp. 37–49.

superficial observer very naturally jumps to the conclusion that the seven modes are merely different segments of one and the same mode, that of C-major.

We see, then, that the early history of Church music justifies to some extent the inference that the sense of modality, which the Ambrosian rule, cited by Helmholtz, would seem to imply, could scarcely have originated with the Church musicians. For, if the Ambrosian system had been of their own invention, they would have appreciated its full significance and jealously preserved it. As, however, they did not preserve it, we can but assume that the Church musicians inherited their musical system from an outside source; and that that system was so far in advance of their musical development that they failed to apprehend its real meaning. As it was from the Greeks, presumably, that the Church learned the rule in question, there is, therefore, some warrant for concluding that the Greeks did, in post-classical days, arrive at an understanding of the meaning of modality.

The modes of S. Ambrose were four in number. These are known as the *authentic* modes or tones, and are distinguished by the odd numbers, 1, 3, 5, and 7, thus:

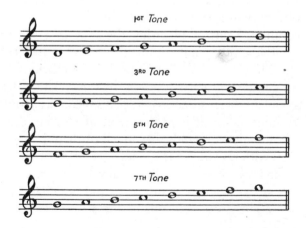

Not one of these scales corresponds with either the major or the modern minor scale. When, however, the B was lowered to Bb, as,

in accordance with later Greek practice, was occasionally permitted, the 5th tone would then coincide with our major scale, and
the 1st tone with our descending melodic minor scale.

To these four tones Gregory added four more, which were
distinguished from the Ambrosian authentic modes by being called
plagal. The plagal modes were numbered 2, 4, 6, and 8, thus:

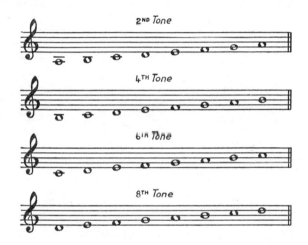

The finals of these four plagal scales were respectively D, E, F,
and G, *i.e.*, the same as those of the four Ambrosian or authentic
modes. The Gregorian plagal modes were, therefore, not new
modes at all, but segments of the older authentic tones, from
which they differed in compass, but not in modality.

The number of Church tones was eventually increased to
fourteen by the addition of three more authentic tones on A, B,
and C, and their corresponding plagals on E, F, and G. The complete list is given on the next page.

Of these, the authentic tone on B and its plagal on F (the 11th and
12th tones), because of the false fifth B—F, were dubbed 'bastard
tones', and excluded from the system. The thirteenth tone, corresponding to our major mode, and its plagal, the fourteenth tone,
were also banned; but for a different reason. The major was the
mode in which so many of the 'ribald ballads' of the people were

cast, and it was, on that account, called the *modus lascivus*, and excluded from ecclesiastical use.

The system of numbering the Church tones still obtains, but amongst secular musicians the old scales are known by the pseudo-Greek names. This mistaken Greek nomenclature was first introduced in 1547 by Glarean, who attempted, in his *Dodecachordon*, to resolve the confusion into which the theory of scales had fallen. His application of the Greek tribal names to the wrong scales suggests that his knowledge of Greek music was not very profound.

Glarean propounded twelve modes of which six were authentic

and six plagal. Unhappily he failed to distinguish between 'accidental' and 'essential' scales, and accounted both plagal and authentic tones as separate and distinct modes. He thus perpetuated the confusion which the introduction of the plagal tones by Pope Gregory a thousand years earlier had initiated. Glarean's twelve tones were the fourteen Church tones, with the omission of the unmelodic eleventh and twelfth tones.

We will now give a table of the fourteen tones, with their Church numbers, their ancient Greek names, and the Greek names, falsely ascribed to them by Glarean, by which they are now known.

Church Tones		Ancient Greek Names	Greek Names by which the Modes are known in England	The Natural or Open Scales
1st Tone	(Authentic)	Phrygian	Dorian	D—D
2nd ,,	(Plagal)		Hypodorian	A—A
3rd ,,	(Authentic)	Dorian	Phrygian	E—E
4th ,,	(Plagal)		Hypophrygian	B—B
5th ,,	(Authentic)	Hypolydian	Lydian	F—F
6th ,,	(Plagal)		Hypolydian	C—C
7th ,,	(Authentic)	Hypophrygian	Mixolydian	G—G
8th ,,	(Plagal)		Hypomixolydian	D—D
9th ,,	(Authentic)	Hypodorian	Aeolian	A—A
10th ,,	(Plagal)		Hypoaeolian	E—E
*11th ,,	(Authentic)	Mixolydian	*Locrian	B—B
*12th ,,	(Plagal)		*Hypolocrian	F—F
13th ,,	(Authentic)	Lydian	Ionian	C—C
14th ,,	(Plagal)		Hypoionian	G—G

* Sometimes omitted, in which case the 13th and 14th Tones were numbered the 11th and 12th

THE MODES IN MODERN MUSIC

The mediaeval modes were used in polyphonic music, both ecclesiastical and secular, down to the close of the first quarter of the seventeenth century. During the last fifty years or so of that period, a change began to take place in the use of the modes, which eventually led to their abandonment, and the substitution in their stead of our modern system of major and minor scales. This change originated from the difficulty which contrapuntists experienced in providing satisfactory harmonies to modal melodies. Musicians found that in certain passages, particularly in the cadences, the ear demanded the introduction of certain notes foreign to the mode. This led to the occasional use of accidentals, which were, however, strictly confined to the subordinate parts, their introduction into the melody itself, or Cantus Firmus, being resolutely forbidden. Out of respect for popular prejudice, musicians, for a half-century or more, refrained from marking these inflections in their scores, relying upon the singers to make the necessary changes—a typical instance of the conservative nature of the artist. The singers were guided by certain unwritten laws, tacitly agreed upon by both composers and performers. The music of this period was called 'musica ficta'.

The fact is that, after the introduction of harmony, musicians found it impossible to obtain a satisfactory cadence, or point of repose, unless one part proceeded to the last chord by the step of a semitone upwards to the tonic. In other words the need of a 'leading note' began to assert itself. As only two of the available modes had leading notes of their own, this necessitated the introduction of accidentals in the remaining four. In melodies without accompaniment, or even in short harmonized compositions, the lack of a leading note was not seriously felt. But in extended compositions, where frequent cadences were necessary to avoid obscurity, it was found impossible to dispense with it.

The ionian and lydian modes each possessed a leading note. It was only necessary to flatten the fourth note of the latter for both modes to become major scales. Raising the seventh of the mixolydian mode reduced that scale also to the major pattern. The remaining three, viz., the dorian, phrygian and aeolian, needed but little alteration, beyond the sharpening of their sevenths, to make them conform to the minor scale. Thus, three of the ancient modes lost their identity in the major scale, while the remaining three became merged in the minor.

The great advance which, in consequence of the extinction of the modes, harmonic music has since made, fully justifies the change.

But it was not all gain; something must be placed to the debit side of the account. As vehicles of pure melody, the ancient modes were far superior to the scales which supplanted them; and lovers of melody, pure and simple, will, for this reason, deplore their loss. It may be that the increasing interest that is now being excited in folk music, especially in that part of it which is modal, may lead to a revival of the ancient modes.[1]

But if the modes are to be brought again into common use, if they are to enrich, and to extend the boundaries of modern music, they must not be regarded as mere varieties or modifications of major and minor scales, but be frankly accepted as genuine modes, possessing each its own character and individuality. Following upon centuries of experience in the manipulation of the major and minor scales, musicians have learned how to treat them as separate and distinct modes, and to preserve the character of each, not by disguising their differences, but by accentuating them. The old difficulty of treating the modes harmonically, which troubled the sixteenth century musicians, and which led eventually to their abandonment, has no longer to be reckoned with. But there is the danger, and a very real one, that the harmonic skill possessed by the modern musician may, where the modes are in question, be used indiscriminately and unwisely.

For, of course, each of the modes has its own set of intervals from which it derives an individuality as characteristic and distinct as that of the major or minor. If, therefore, the modes are to take their place side by side with the major and minor scales, it must be on equal terms, and as separate and distinct systems, possessing specific qualities of their own.

The character of every melody is, in part, derived from the mode in which it is cast. Consequently, new modes should give birth to new types of melody. This they have already done in the mouths of the folk; and this they will also do in the hands of musicians, if they are treated with a wise restraint, sympathetically, and with a due appreciation of their especial musical qualities and capabilities.

It is so easy to harmonize a modal melody in terms of major or

[1] It can, indeed, be said that this has taken place.

minor; and also, of course, the quickest and most effectual way of destroying its modal character. Unfortunately, too, this is the treatment that in nine cases out of ten it will receive from the modern musician—and not perhaps unnaturally. He is so saturated in the harmonic effects which are peculiar to the major and minor system, that they dominate his thoughts and colour everything that he writes. Every passage of music that comes his way he refers, as of instinct, to the modern tonality. It is not that he is necessarily antipathetic to the modes, but that he fails to perceive that they call for any special treatment. They come to him as remnants of a dead past that need modern handling if they are to be revivified and made acceptable to modern ears. He underestimates their musical and emotional capabilities, and, by disguising their essential and characteristic qualities, he robs them of all that is individual. In the result he produces a hybrid which is neither major, minor, nor modal.

If he were to go down into the country, seek out the old peasant singers, and hear modal tunes sung by those to whom the modes are the natural scales, he would understand what is meant by the specific musical qualities of the various modes. He would get rid, once for all, of the idea that modal music has no message for the modern ear; that the modes are merely archaic survivals, of no present value whatever, except for manufacturing what are commonly known as 'Wardour Street effects'. He would, on the contrary, derive from the modal folk tune a definite musical impression, fundamentally different from any that he had hitherto experienced. He would, assuredly, yield to its fascination and realize that the modes really offered a new channel of musical expression, and an escape from the present restricted tonality. There is a world of difference between a dead language and a living one.

When, after this experience, he came to harmonize a modal folk tune, he would instinctively strive, by carefully chosen harmonies, to preserve and translate into terms of polyphony that peculiar modal quality which had so impressed him. And this he would find to be quite possible; but only so long as he eschewed modulations to major and minor scales, and kept rigidly within the tonality of its mode. He would not, for instance, harmonize an aeolian air partly in the modern minor scale with a sharpened seventh and partly in the relative major. Nor would he treat his mixolydian tunes with sharpened leading notes and frequent modulations to the major scale of the subdominant; nor his dorian melodies as though they were minor tunes, perpetually modulating to the dominant minor scale—and so forth. Rather would he confine himself, at first at any rate, exclusively to the notes of the mode, and seek to realize and to feel the relative values and specific qualities of its seven diatonic common chords.

That Beethoven was keenly alive to the musical significance of the modes he has shown in his harmonization of the 'Sacred Song in the Lydian Mode', in the quartet No. 15, Op. 132. The melody is harmonized exclusively with diatonic chords of the mode and without, of course, modulation. This is a typical example of genuine modal writing, and one which musicians would do well to study.

BEETHOVEN QUARTET   Op. 132

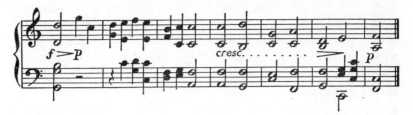

Needless to say, modal folk airs have suffered grievously at the hands of modern musicians. Curiously enough, Brahms, who had the deepest affection for folk music, is one of the worst offenders. This is particularly unfortunate, for Brahams is regarded by musicians of the present generation, and justly so, with the deepest reverence; and this makes it extremely difficult to win a hearing for views that conflict with his teaching.

Of the modal airs included in his seven books of *German Folk-Songs* (Simrock), there is not one that is harmonized in its own mode. In every case the mode is ignored, frankly, and no doubt with set intention; the melody is referred to more than one tonic, and treated as a hybrid tune, a patchwork of major and minor modes and keys.

The following is a typical example of the harmonic scheme adopted by Brahms:

DER REITER

Harmonized by Johannes Brahms

The notes of which this melody is composed (excluding the D-sharp in the eighth bar, which is an auxiliary note), form the following scale:

This is, of course, the aeolian mode, in the key of A. Brahms has, nevertheless, harmonized it partly in the modern minor key of A, with a sharpened G, and partly in the relative major scale of C. The G-natural, which occurs in the melody six times, is throughout treated, not as the seventh note of the aeolian scale of A, but as the fifth degree of the major scale of C. The introduction of a leading note, where none exists in the melody, and the reference to two tonics and two modes, to neither of which the melody belongs, not only destroy its tonality, but deprive the air of all of its most characteristic elements.

There are seven more aeolian airs in the same collection, Nos. 7, 17, 22, 24, 16, 30 and 31, and they are all harmonized upon what I venture to call a faulty and illogical principle, *i.e.* as minor airs, eked out with modulations to the relative major key.

Nos. 9 and 10 are both phrygian airs in the key of F-sharp, but they are treated as major melodies in the key of D, ending on the third notes of their scales; while the dorian tune, No. 14, is harmonized partly in the tonic minor, and partly in the dominant minor.

To refer a simple folk air like any one of these to two or more tonal centres can only obscure its tonality and cloud its meaning. Mere craftmanship, however clever, even when it is masterly as that of Brahms, cannot convert a method which is radically unsound into a good one. As a general principle, too, modulating harmonies are out of place in the accompaniment to a folk song. For, as we shall see in the next chapter, folk airs very rarely the modulate; spirit of modulation is foreign to them.

Many writers have consistently followed the example set by Brahms, and have harmonized their modal folk airs in modern and non-modal fashion. Few, however, of his imitators are equipped with a like technique; consequently, in their hands the faults of the method become magnified.[1]

The best modern examples of the harmonization of modal folk airs are, perhaps, to be seen in M. Bourgault-Ducoudray's *Mélodies Populaires de Grèce*, and his *Mélodies Populaires de Basse-Bretagne*. M. Ducoudray recites his modal creed in the preface to the former of these two volumes in the following sentences:

> We have made it a rule never to alter the melody for the sake of the harmony; on the contrary we have made the harmony conform to the melody, and have forced ourselves to preserve in the accompaniment the character of the mode in which the melody is cast. . . . In the work of harmonization we have not banned the use of any harmonic

---

[1] Sharp gives an example of such a harmonization by an unspecified composer, but since it adds little to the argument we have omitted it. We have also omitted an alternative arrangement of *Der Reiter* by Cecil Sharp himself in which we feel he has failed to do himself justice.

combination. The only harmonies that we have proscribed are those which seemed to conflict with the modal impression created by the melody that was to be harmonized. We have directed our efforts to enlarge the circle of the modalities of polyphonic music, and not to restrict the resources of modern harmony. We have declined to be bound by the rules of a past age in an attempt which is new; if it is to find imitators the future must prove.

We trust that we have been able to show that the application of harmony to Oriental scales is productive of result. Eastern music, till now exclusively melodic, will start upon a new harmonic career; Western harmonic music, hitherto restricted to the exclusive use of two modes, the major and minor, will escape at last from its long confinement. The fruit of this deliverance will be to provide Western musicians with fresh resources of expression, and with colours hitherto unknown to the palette of the musician.

As to how far M. Ducoudray has succeeded in these his efforts to extend the boundaries of modern music, opinions will probably differ. He has, however, shown, and that without question, that it is possible to draw upon the resources of a modern technique in the harmonization of modal folk airs, and yet retain their essential modal characteristics.

It is interesting, too, to note that M. Ducoudray makes it the test of good harmonization that the effect shall accord with the 'modal impression created by the melody'. He had, of course, himself collected the songs that he harmonized, so that in his case that 'modal impression' was the result of actual experience. And this, as I have already suggested, is the best education that the musician can undergo, the surest way of bringing about his conversion. For the pioneer, it is probably the only way.[1]

PENTATONIC SCALE[2]

The pentatonic scale (five notes to the octave) is widely distributed in the folk music of the present day, and it is to be found in

---

[1] Since this chapter was written, many fine and satisfying harmonizations of modal folk tunes have been published. Apart from Cecil Sharp's own arrangements, those of Vaughan Williams, Gustav Holst and George Butterworth may be cited.

[2] This section has been re-written in the light of Cecil Sharp's later views.

the traditional art music of many oriental countries. We know also that it was practised in ancient times, notably by the Chinese and the Greeks.

In the form in which it is most familiar to western ears, it possesses no semitone, the intervals between the notes consisting of whole tones and one-and-a-half tones. It can be played on the white notes of the pianoforte, eliminating E and B, or, alternatively, on the black notes.

According to the relative position of the tonic, there are five pentatonic modes, *i.e.*:

The tonic of a pentatonic mode is, however, often not so well defined as that of a heptatonic (seven-note) scale. For that reason some scholars prefer not to differentiate between the modes of the pentatonic scale, but to regard them as segments of the same scale.

Cecil Sharp supported the theory that the seven-note diatonic scale is a development of the pentatonic scale, in which the 'missing' notes are filled in by one or other of the following combinations: E♭ and B♭, E♮ and B♭, E♮ and B♮. In the transition from the pentatonic to the heptatonic scale the medial notes are introduced with some uncertainty, that is, they are used merely as passing or auxiliary notes, or they are indeterminate in pitch, or they vary from major to minor.[1] In English folk song the third, sixth and seventh are often so affected.

In the folk songs that have been recovered in England there are but few instances of pure pentatonic tunes. There are, however, a number of hexatonic (six-note) tunes, usually with the sixth missing. This and the occurrence of 'weak' or 'indeterminate' notes may be an indication of their pentatonic ancestry.

The pentatonic scale is common in Scotland, particularly in the tunes which accompany the Gaelic songs; and a large proportion of the tunes which Cecil Sharp collected in the Southern Appalachian Mountains of America are pentatonic (see pp. x–xi). Pentatonic tunes are also to be found in other regions of North American and in Ireland.

Cecil Sharp suggested two theories to account for the pentatonic character of the Appalachian tunes. The first was based on the assumption that the songs originally came from the North of England or the English-speaking regions of Scotland and that by propinquity they may have been influenced by the pentatonic music of the Scottish Gaels. The second theory, which on the whole he thought the more likely, was that the pentatonic was an earlier form of scale and that it had been in common use among the English peasantry at the time that the ancestors of the mountain people left the country.

Pentatonic and hexatonic scales are commonly referred to as 'gapped' scales, but this term, though convenient, is misleading, because it implies incompleteness, which is not the case. A tune cast in a five-note scale is as complete as one which uses seven notes.

[1] For a fuller exposition, see Sharp & Karpeles: *English Folk-Songs from the Southern Appalachians*, pp. xix–xx and xxx–xxxiv. See also Bronson: *Traditional Tunes*, I, p. 52, II, p. xii.

CHAPTER VI

ENGLISH FOLK SCALES

ENGLISH FOLK TUNES are cast in the dorian, phrygian, mixolydian, aeolian, and ionian (major) modes, and occasionally in the minor. Personally, I have never recovered an English folk tune in the minor scale, and very few have been recorded by other collectors. Minor folk airs are, no doubt, aeolian airs that have been modernized by the addition of a leading note. The minor is a very modern scale in art music, and lends itself more readily to harmonic effects than to melodic.

This large preponderance of aeolian over minor airs is very remarkable; it is, I believe, peculiar to English folk song.[1] The explanation may be that the influence of modern music has extended further and more thoroughly into the remote districts of European countries than has been the case in England. Or it may be that European collections of folk songs have been more freely edited than ours. The cultivated musician cannot rid himself of the notion that a scale with a minor seventh is fundamentally false, and conflicts with natural law. When, therefore, he is confronted with folk tunes containing flattened sevenths he hastily concludes, either that they have been wrongly recorded, or that they are the ignorant corruptions of rude singers. In either case, he feels himself justified in raising the sevenths in accordance with his modern ideas. It should be remembered that of the two melodic forms of the minor scale, the descending is identical with the aeolian mode, while the ascending form does not coincide with any one of the modes, and is not, strictly speaking, a diatonic scale.

The phrygian mode occurs but rarely in English folk song. I do not think that more than half a dozen English folk airs in that mode have been recorded.

So far as I am aware, no English collector has yet found a folk

[1] In view of recent scientific collection in Europe this view cannot be upheld.

tune in the lydian mode.[1] I have, however, occasionally noticed a tendency, more particularly amongst fiddlers, to sharpen the fourth note of the major scale, and it is possible that this may be due to lydian influence. The English folk singer, to judge by his tunes, is very sensitive to the harsh effect of the tritone, which, of course, is the characteristic interval of the lydian mode.

The majority of our English folk tunes, say two-thirds, are in the major or ionian mode. The remaining third is fairly evenly divided between the mixolydian, dorian and aeolian modes, with, perhaps, a preponderance in favour of the mixolydian. These figures have been compiled from an examination of my own collection; but I believe they accord approximately with the experiences of other collectors.

It is not necessary to attribute this large proportion of ionian tunes to modern influence, for the folk have always shown a special predilection for that mode. It was, indeed, because of its popularity with the common people that the Church dubbed it the *modus lascivus,* and prohibited it from use in the Divine Office. It will be remembered, too, that one of the earliest known song-tunes, 'Sumer is icumen in', is cast in this mode.

With many folk-singers the proportion of modal songs is much larger than one third; indeed, some of them sing almost exclusively in the modes. Only last winter, for instance, I sat one day from noon till four o'clock in the parlour of a primitive wayside inn on the peat moors of Somerset. The company numbered on the average some twelve or fourteen men and song followed song in quick succession, but not a single major or minor tune was sung throughout the whole of the four hours.

This partiality for the modes on the part of the English peasant-singer is a fact that is by no means generally known amongst English musicians, as the following quotation from a class-singing book, recently published, will prove:

English children may at first experience some difficulty in grasping the peculiar scales and intervals of Keltic tunes; but what Scotch, Welsh,

[1] Cecil Sharp subsequently noted a tune in the lydian mode: 'James MacDonald', which he obtained from a gipsy singer (see *F.S.F.S.,* IV, No. 103).

and Irish children can sing naturally, English children can acquire, and the trouble will be amply repaid by the widening of their musical horizon, and by the more deeply poetical influence which Keltic music will exert upon the young mind.

As a fact, and one to which I can personally testify, English children sing in the mixolydian, aeolian and dorian modes with the utmost ease. It is, after all, only natural that they should do so, seeing that their ancestors have always shown a marked preference for those modes. Mr Perceval Graves has come to the same conclusion. In the very able address which he delivered to the Welsh Folk-Song Society, he remarked that 'to suggest that England and Wales were distinguished from the Irish and Scots by not using modal tunes at an early period is preposterous.'

It is often said, too, that the introduction of plain-song into the services of the English Church should never be attempted, save only in those town and city churches where the congregations are of educated people. This is surely an error. Cultivated people who have been brought up on modern music will only acquire the art of modal singing with effort and difficulty; to many of them, the Gregorian tones, with their flattened sevenths and unexpected intervals, will never sound natural or convincing. On the other hand, the congregations of village churches will take to plain-song much more readily, and to the manner born. For the Gregorian tones are their own scales, in which for generations past their forbears have been accustomed to sing. The flattened seventh possesses no terrors for the country singer. The leading note is much more likely to cause him difficulty. Who has not heard the village organist struggling to force the sharpened seventh, especially of tunes in the minor mode, upon the unwilling ears of a rustic congregation?

The identification of mode is simple enough if we take the final note of a melody to be its tonic. For then it is enough to examine the second, third, sixth, and seventh notes of the scale to arrive at the mode. If, for instance, all of these notes are minor, the mode is phrygian. If, however, the second is major and the others minor, the mode is aeolian—and so forth (see pp. 48–50). Whether or not we are justified in always assuming the concluding note of a tune to be its tonic is, perhaps, a moot point. Some will think that to do so is to beg the question.

Now, definiteness of tonality requires, as we have already seen, that the tonic shall be supreme throughout the melody. A conclusion on the tonic is the most effective way of accentuating this supremacy; but, of itself, it is not enough. For, unless the tonic is felt, throughout, to be the link connecting the several notes of the melody, the concluding note will come as a surprise and will lack the feeling of naturalness and inevitability. The performance of a well-designed melody should leave the hearer with a sense of complete repose, and this effect will be wanting unless the melody converges simply and naturally to its conclusion. In other words, the melody must not only end on the tonic; it must also be dominated throughout by that note.[1]

This is especially necessary in the case of an unaccompanied melody. In harmonized music the tonality may be defined by the underlying chords, and there is then not the same need for a frequent reference, actual or implied, to the tonic in the melody itself. Such a melody may even conclude on the third or fifth notes of the scale without disguising the tonality, so long as its final note is harmonized with the chord of the tonic.

But, it may be objected, there is no such thing as an intelligible melody that has no relation to harmony; that it is impossible to think a melody without thinking a harmony to it. This is true for us, no doubt, but it is certainly not true for the average folk singer. We must remember that scales were in use centuries before harmony was thought of; and that history shows that the art of accompanying a tune with even the simplest chords was acquired very slowly and with, apparently, the utmost difficulty. An analysis of ancient popular melodies, too, seems to show that they were composed without reference to harmony; indeed some of them will

[1] This statement is puzzling, for it appears to be contradicted by the example of 'Sweet Kitty' (see pp. 76–7) and to Sharp's reference on p.108 to 'a certain vagueness of tonality, especially in the opening phrases of modal tunes'.

only admit of an accompaniment by the exercise of great ingenuity.

My own experience has taught me that with the folk singers of today the sense of harmony is very rudimentary. It was only very few of them, for instance, who were able to recognize their own songs when I played harmonized versions of them on the piano; and still fewer who could sing them to the simplest instrumental accompaniment. The average folk singer of today stands, I believe, with regard to harmony just where his more cultivated predecessor stood in pre-harmonic days. Otherwise, he would long ago have exchanged his non-harmonic melodies for modern harmonic tunes, or have modified them in accordance with the modern feeling for harmony. I do not say that this has not to some extent taken place; nor, again, will I affirm that every folk tune is non-harmonic. The harmonic sense reflected by those tunes that have not been corrupted by modern influence is, however, very elementary. Moreover, the fact, as we have already seen, that the peasant singer still sings a large number of modal melodies in-dicates a preference for the non-harmonic tune; for the modes are essentially melodic and not harmonic scales. I have never heard old singing men attempt to sing in parts. The only concerted music the countryman ever hears is at the village church on Sundays. The old men, who used to play stringed or wind instruments in church, may, perhaps, have developed some sense of harmony. But then, they do not sing in the modes—at least, none of those that I have come across.

The fact, too, that a folk tune so rarely modulates that one can almost say that it never modulates at all, provides further evidence pointing to the same direction. Change of mode, or rather the inflection of a note which may or may not imply a change of mode, is met with in English folk song; but this very rarely involves a change of tonic such as is implied by a change of key. The folk singer has not even developed that elementary feeling for harmony which demands a modulation to the dominant at the middle cadence of a major tune. He will, on the contrary, go out of his way to avoid it. The well-known tune of 'Polly Oliver', which in the received version modulates to the dominant in the following way:

POLLY OLIVER

From Chappell's Popular Music

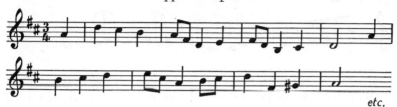

etc.

has always been sung to me in some such way as this:

POLLY OLIVER

etc.

The disinclination of the folk singer to modulate in such a case as this is all the more remarkable, because what feeling for harmony he may have would be shown in a major tune more readily than in one in any other mode.

I will now give an example of a modal tune, which conveys but little sense of an underlying harmony, but in which, nevertheless, the tonality is clearly defined:

HIGH GERMANY

First version

AEOLIAN

It will be seen that this tune begins on the chord of C, the seventh note of the scale, and that the tonic is not defined until the fourth bar. A large number of modal folk tunes begin in this unusual way, i.e. with a note that is not the tonic, and with a phrase which is not suggestive of the tonic harmony. Indeed, this unconventional beginning is highly characteristic of the folk tune; and it is, I believe, the direct outcome of the peculiar conditions under which it has been evolved. We must remember that the folk singer habitually sings without accompaniment, and that his mind is engrossed with the words of his song rather than with its tune, which to him is a matter of secondary importance. Now, a pause at the end of every verse would, in the absence of an accompaniment, be peculiarly tiresome and senseless, and would materially interfere with the continuity of the narrative. Both considerations urge the folk singer to sing his ballad straight through, without pause; and this, of course, is his invariable habit. In practice, therefore, the first phrase of a folk tune follows immediately upon the conclusion of the last one. Now, if the key were to be defined with equal clearness both at the beginning and at the end of the melody, the first phrase would have the effect of a repetition of the last one, rather than a continuation of it; and this would obstruct the even flow of the melody. Accordingly, the opening phrase, especially of ballad-tunes, has come to be evolved in a form which will fit in naturally and continuously with the concluding strain of the air.

In an art song, on the other hand, it is customary to separate the verses with a few bars of accompaniment, and to end each verse with a decided cadence. The cultivated singer, moreover, thinks more of his tune and less of his words than the folk singer, and attaches but slight importance to maintaining the continuity of his narrative. There is nothing, therefore, to deter the composer from defining both key and mode in the opening bars of his melody. This may not be the invariable practice in very modern music, but in the composed music of fifty years and more ago it would be difficult to find a melody which could not be accompanied with the harmony of the tonic in its opening bar.

To return, however, to the tune under discussion. The whole of the first phrase of 'High Germany' provides an excellent example of a non-harmonic melody. The first two bars, for instance, are not easy to harmonize, because of the non-harmonic way in which the passing notes C and G are used.

I have collected a variant of this air which begins in a more usual manner:

Second version

AEOLIAN

etc.

and my friend, Mr H. E. D. Hammond, has noted down yet another variant in Dorset.

Third version[1]

AEOLIAN

etc.

In both these versions the tonic is clearly defined in the first bar, and again at the beginning of the fourth; indeed, in the Dorset variant, the first four bars could be harmonized with the tonic chord alone. I venture to think, however, that the tonality of the first version is quite as clearly defined as it is in either of the other two.

[1] *English County Folk Songs*, I. p. 12.

In the next example, that of 'Sweet Kitty'—a dorian tune—the tonality is less clear.

SWEET KITTY[1]

First version

It must be confessed that the conclusion of this tune comes upon the ear as a surprise. G would seem to have been the natural note to end with; for the tune begins with that note, and all the cadences fall upon one or other of the notes of the chord of G minor. As the tune stands, it leaves behind it a sense of vagueness and lack of completion. Many folk tunes are like 'Sweet Kitty' in this respect, and I can only assume that either folk singers like this effect or, at least, do not object to it. For my own part, I do not find that tunes of this kind repel me, although, when I first heard them, they struck me as very curious and unusual. In a variant of this air, in the same mode, which I noted at Minehead, and which I now print, the tonality is quite clear.

Second version

1 *Selected Edition,* I, p. 90.

Some critics may consider that the first tune is but a corrupt version of the second, which they will look upon as the original. I have already shown that we cannot regard any version of a folk tune as the 'original'; but, apart from this, I believe that many folk singers would prefer the first tune to the second.

At any rate, the fact that the folk do sing such tunes as 'Sweet Kitty' without hesitation or incorrect intonation is of itself proof that they find in this type of tune a satisfactory medium of self-expression. The earlier folk tune may well have been of a simpler type, fashioned on a pattern more easy of comprehension than the one in question. In art music it is the genius only who can success-fully violate rule. He is the pioneer, who shows the way for others to follow, each generation thus making rules to be broken by the next. Folk music has developed in like manner, except for the fact that its growth has been spontaneous, unconscious, and un-perceived. 'Sweet Kitty' may, therefore, be the product of a late rather than an early stage of development.

There are some folk tunes whose vagueness of conclusion admits of another and simpler explanation. These may be called 'circular' tunes, in that they are intended to be played over and over again. The apparent end of a circular tune is not the real one, but is designed to lead back to the first phrase without break. The well-known dance tune 'Dargason' may be cited as an example.

DARGASON

From Chappell's Popular Music

When a tune is played as an accompaniment to the dance, it is, of course, repeated as often as the dancers require it. If, therefore, a dance tune, beginning with a tonic phrase, were also to end with the usual full close on the tonic, the music would be a succession of full-stops; and this would be very tiresome and disconcerting to the dancers. In ballad tunes, as we have already seen, a similar difficulty was obviated by a free treatment of the opening phrase. But in dance music the converse of this method was the more usual. That is to say, the concluding phrase was changed, the final cadence avoided, and an ending substituted that would dovetail naturally into the beginning of the air, and thus allow the repetition to be effected without break of continuity. The full close would then be postponed until the conclusion of the dance, and the player would, consequently, play the false cadence very many times, while the proper conclusion would occur but once. In this way, the latter would tend to fall into disuse and to be forgotten. Consequently, many dance tunes have come down to us in an incomplete form, shorn of their proper endings. A certain number of song tunes, too, if often used as dance airs, would be corrupted in like manner, and be perpetuated in an incomplete form. The following, I take it, is such a one (see *F.S.J.* II, p. 97):

THE TWO AFFECTIONATE LOVERS

Noted by F. Gwillim

The cadence to this tune may have been either

'Queen Jean' (*F.S.J.* II, p. 221) is another instance of a circular tune.

The Gregorian tones to which the psalms are sometimes chanted in the English Church are also incomplete tunes, like the circular dance airs which we have just been considering. In primitive days it was customary for the people to sing a refrain or antiphon, consisting of a few words of scripture, between each verse of the psalm. The music, to verse and refrain together, made one continuous melody, the full close of which came at the conclusion of the antiphon. Later on, the practice of singing the antiphon between each verse of the psalm fell into disuse, and the refrain was only sung once, after the last verse of the psalm. This practice still obtains in the Roman Church, but in the Anglican Communion the antiphon has disappeared altogether. Consequently the Gregorian psalm tones, as they are sung in England, are, like circular dance airs, incomplete tunes which have been deprived of their last phrases, and which never attain to a full close.

Besides 'circular' tunes there are other folk airs which apparently, conclude on notes other than the tonic.

I have in my collection a few tunes in the aeolian mode which end on the third of the scale. Here is one of them:

THE HEARTY GOOD FELLOW

If the last note of this tune is the tonic, the melody is in the key of G major. But the character of the tune is definitely aeolian rather than major, as any one would discover who tried to harmonize it (see *Songs of the West*, No. 26). This cannot be a corrupt tune, because I have taken down numerous variants of it, and all of them end in the same way. It belongs to a class of tune, therefore, which conflicts with the usual rule that a folk tune always concludes upon the tonic. 'The Farmer's Daughter' (*F.S.F.S.* II No. 50) is another instance of the same peculiarity. The German folk song *All mein Gedanken*, harmonized by Brahms, is yet another example.[1]

Again, there are a few folk tunes which, judging by their finals, are mixolydian, but which are, nevertheless, major rather than mixolydian in character. I have always suspected the cadences to these tunes to be corrupt and due to the imperfect recollection of the singers, and the other day a case occurred which confirmed my suspicions. I was noting down from a peasant woman the following tune to 'The Unquiet Grave':

THE UNQUIET GRAVE

First version

The conclusion to this air seemed to me to be very peculiar and unexpected. Although, strictly speaking, it was mixolydian, yet I felt sure the tune was really a major one. I accordingly prevailed upon the singer to repeat the ballad several times. When she had sung the air ten or twenty times, she suddenly repeated the last line of one of the verses to the following phrase:

[1] German folk tunes frequently end on the mediant. It has been suggested that this may possibly be due to the practice of singing in thirds, thus allowing the second voice to finish on the tonic.

I have no doubt but that this was the correct form of the tune, and that in her previous repetitions the singer had forgotten to 'double' the last line. The tune was, after all, a major one in the key of G; not a mixolydian in D, as it at first appeared to be.

This is the only experience of the kind that I have as yet met with, and it is, perhaps, not safe to generalize on such slender evidence. Nevertheless, I have a strong suspicion that not a few folk tunes which appear to be mixolydian are, in reality, incomplete major tunes. It is not difficult to detect them to one who is familiar with the modes.

There are, then, three classes of tunes in which it is not always safe to regard the final note as tonic.

(1) 'Circular' tunes.
(2) Aeolian airs ending on the third of the scale.
(3) Major airs with false mixolydian endings.

The non-harmonic character of many folk tunes is exemplified by the notes of the scale upon which the several divisions or cadences fall. In harmonic melodies, the note at the midway cadence is usually the dominant, or a note of the dominant harmony. In major folk tunes this is very frequently the case, e.g., the following example:

HARES ON THE MOUNTAINS[1]

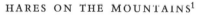

[1] *Selected Edition*, I, p. 108.

The mid-cadence will, however, often fall on the third or sixth notes of the scale. We have already seen an example of the use of the sixth for this purpose in 'Polly Oliver' (see p. 73). Of the seven notes of the major scale, the sixth, perhaps, suggests harmony the least of all. The seventh, when it is a leading note, brings to mind the dominant harmony; the fourth, that of the sub-dominant, and so on. But the sixth, if it suggests anything at all, suggests a modulation to the relative minor. For this reason Sir Hubert Parry (*Art of Music*, p. 49) describes the submediant as 'the most indefinite note in the system'. The folk singer does not find it indefinite, but this is because he is thinking in terms of melody, not of harmony.

To dwell on the mediant at a pause or cadence is a very favourite device with the folk singer, and one that he often uses with very happy effect, as in the following very beautiful tune:

THE CRYSTAL SPRING[1]

In modal tunes the seventh note often marks the cadence, especially in mixolydian tunes, as in the following examples:

I'M SEVENTEEN COME SUNDAY

First version

MIXOLYDIAN

[1] *Selected Edition*, II, p. 42 and *Folk Songs for Schools*, No. 952 (Set 1).

THE UNQUIET GRAVE

Second version

In the modes, the seventh note plays a much more important part than it does in the modern scales, where it is a leading note, and suggestive of the dominant harmony. In the second version of 'High Germany' already quoted (see p. 75), the cadences fall alternately on the tonic and the seventh note, and the latter note is constantly referred to throughout the tune. There is also another example of the same thing in 'Bruton Town' (see p. 31).

Sir Hubert Parry, in the chapter on Scales in his *Art of Music*, points out that 'in melodic systems the influence of vocal music is infinitely paramount; in modern European art the instrumental element is strongest.' In illustration of this, he shows that modern melodies, in rising to the last note of the concluding cadence, do so for harmonic considerations only. The natural instinct is for the voice to fall to the cadence, as the word implies, and this is almost invariably the case in modal melodies. If the reader will examine the examples of modal tunes quoted in this book he will find that this is so—but with this further qualification. The downward phrase will often descend below the tonic, to the seventh note of the scale, and then return to the key-note, *e.g.*

This use of the flattened seventh, as though it were a leading note, is often to be found in folk airs, especially in those of England. The modern musician finds, in this practice, that which is so directly at variance with all that he believes to be natural, that I have known him to question the fact that folk singers really do sing such phrases. They do, however, and the effect is often very beautiful. Musicians forget that what they call a 'natural' desire for a leading note is no more than a desire for what they have been accustomed to hear. The sharpened seventh is no more and no less 'natural' than the flattened seventh. Nature has nothing whatever to do with the matter, one way or the other; it is purely a question of habit or convention.

MODULATION

Modulation may be effected in three ways:

(1) By change of key without change of mode, *e.g.*, C-major to F-major, or G-minor to D-minor.

(2) By change of key together with change of mode, *e.g.*, C-major to A-minor, or G-mixolydian to D-dorian.

(3) By change of mode without change of key, *e.g.*, C-major to C-minor, or A-dorian to A-phrygian.

When we remember that there was, generally speaking, no modulation in art music until after the close of the polyphonic period, *i.e.*, c. 1625, it is not surprising that, as already mentioned, folk airs modulate with extreme rarity.

The first of the above forms of modulation may be said to be almost unknown in genuine folk music. Dr Vaughan Williams has, however, pointed out (*F.S.J.* II, p. 198) that there are a few folk airs which convey to modern ears a faint suggestion of a change of tonic, and he cites the following as a case in point:

SALISBURY PLAIN

Third version   *Noted by Dr Vaughan Williams*

This air would be an aeolian tune throughout, were it not for the B-natural in the fifth bar. The inflected note may be interpreted in two ways. It may be regarded as effecting a modulation of the third species, that is a change of mode, aeolian to dorian, without a change of tonic. Or, on the other hand, it may be taken to imply a change of tonal centre, from D to A, without change of mode, in which case it would come under the heading of the first species of modulation. Dr Vaughan Williams is probably right in favouring the latter interpretation, but the matter is by no means free from doubt.

We must remember that progress in the technique of an art takes place very slowly and by very minute steps. We may presume, therefore, that the sense of modulation was manifested vaguely, and in isolated instances, for a long period before it became established and recognized as a principle. The above tune may, therefore, represent an early and, of course, an entirely unconscious effort at modulation, the first foreshadowings of a new departure.

In any case, those tunes which suggest, however faintly, a change of tonal centre are exceedingly rare in folk music. For all practical purposes we may, therefore, eliminate the first two of the above-mentioned species and confine our attention to the third, *i.e.*, change of mode without change of key.

Even modulations of this nature are very unusual in folk music, if we except those doubtful cases of modulation from mixolydian to dorian, and vice versa, which will presently be discussed. With regard to English folk airs in particular, it may be taken, as a general statement, that they never change their key or their mode.[1]

[1] The statement that English folk airs never change their mode is open to question, and Sharp himself points to the phenomenon of mixolydian–dorian tunes (see pp. 87 ff.). We believe that he later modified his views in the light of his experience of pentatonic tunes (see p. 65) and that he would have regarded certain tunes with inflected notes, i.e. the third,

This, however, is not to say that accidentals never occur in English modal folk melodies. They do, of course; but they are, as a rule, auxiliary or passing notes, which induce neither change of key nor change of mode. In the following example, for instance, the B-flat in the penultimate bar is clearly a chromatic auxiliary note; the singer has instinctively preferred the smooth B-flat to the B-natural, which in this place would be very harsh.

I'M SEVENTEEN COME SUNDAY[1]

Second version

Some singers are so possessed by the mode that even in such a case as this they would prefer the modal note. This is exemplified in the next illustration where, except for the B-natural, the passage is almost identical with the corresponding one in the last example:

THE HUSBANDMAN AND THE SERVING MAN

In like manner, the seventh in aeolian airs is occasionally raised a semitone, *i.e.*, as a chromatic auxiliary note; just as the sixth in dorian melodies is sometimes lowered a semitone.

---

sixth or seventh, as being of indeterminate mode, if not bi-modal. In this connection the reader is referred to Percy Grainger's interesting article on 'Folk-Song Scales in the Phonograph' (*F.S.J.* III, 156–9) and to the works of B. H. Bronson cited on p. 53.

[1] *Selected Edition*, I, p. 104.

Theorists will, no doubt, differ in their interpretation of the accidentals which occur in modal folk melodies; and they will not all agree with the explanation above suggested. M. Bourgault-Ducoudray, for instance, in his *Trente Mélodies de Basse-Bretagne*, propounds a modulation whenever a note of a modal tune is inflected. In the following air, for example,

LAMENTATIONS

he points out that the first part of the tune is dorian, and the second half aeolian. I cannot agree with this analysis. The tune appears to me to be dorian throughout, and the B-flat an auxiliary note, which induces no modulation. Of course, if M. Ducoudray's method of analysis be accepted, then the statement that English folk airs rarely modulate will need material modification. That is a matter for theorists to decide.

There are, however, several English folk airs in which accidentals occur that cannot be explained in this way. These are mixolydian tunes in which the third of the scale is occasionally flattened, thus, technically at any rate, changing the mode from mixolydian to dorian. There is no question here of change of key or tonal centre, although it may, possibly, be a case of change of mode. English mixolydian folk tunes will often begin with a dorian phrase, as in the following air,

BARBARA ELLEN

afterwards continuing strictly in the mode. A very remarkable instance of this is exhibited in the following air:

DOWN IN THE GROVES

This is in the mixolydian mode, in the key of C, although the distinctive seventh—in this case B-flat—only occurs in the last bar but one. The flattened third, E-flat, in the last bar, produces a very curious and unexpected effect, and, technically, changes the mode from mixolydian to dorian.

Here is another example very similar to the last one:

AS I WALKED THROUGH THE MEADOWS[1]

First version

[1] *Selected Edition*, I, p. 28.

The last phrase of this air recalls the corresponding phrase in the previous example. The B-natural in the third bar is an inflection obviously introduced for vocal reasons. It is a chromatic auxiliary note and does not induce change of mode.

It would be difficult, I think, to argue that the flattening of the third note of the scale has brought about a modulation from mixolydian to dorian in any one of the three examples just given. They all strike me as mixolydian tunes, not dorian.

This inflection of the third in mixolydian and dorian airs is the only constant and systematic instance of an apparent change of mode to be found in English folk tunes.[1]

It is possible to attribute it to Church influence. For in Church music the B might, on occasion, be changed to B-flat—the only note in the system where this was allowed. Now, in the open scale of the mixolydian mode, with tonic G, the third note of the scale is this same B. So that folk singers in making this inflection are, at any rate, conforming to the practice of the Church. But this, I am satisfied, is not the true explanation. In the first place, although the Church musician dipped freely enough into the people's music, there is very little evidence of any traffic in the reverse direction. The Church musicians were the importers, not the exporters.[2] It is, therefore, extremely unlikely that the people derived this melodic irregularity from ecclesiastical sources. The real explanation must be sought elsewhere.

It must be understood that the third is not a fixed note in the folk scale, as it is in both of the modern scales. The English folk singer varies the intonation of this particular note very considerably. His major third is never as sharp as the corresponding interval in the tempered scale, to which modern ears are attuned. On the other hand, it is often so flat that it is hardly to be distinguished from the minor third. Frequently, too, it is a 'neutral' third, i.e., neither major nor minor, like the interval between the two notes of the

---

[1] The inflection of the sixth in dorian/aeolian tunes and the seventh in ionan/mixolydian tunes should also be added.

[2] This statement is perhaps too dogmatic. Although the balance of indebtedness may be in favour of the Church musicians who drew on the music of the people, it seems hardly likely that there was no influence in the other direction.

cuckoo's song, when the spring is waning. Apparently, the folk singer, not having any settled notions with regard to the pitch of the third note of the scale, varies it according to the character of the phrase in which it happens to occur. The third of the scale may, therefore, be sung with two or even three different shades of intonation in the same tune, not arbitrarily but systematically, *i.e.*, consistently in every verse.

Now the third of the scale is the only note by which the dorian mode may be distinguished from the mixolydian. In the latter it is major; in the former, minor. The folk singer, in either of these two modes, can, therefore, alter his third from major to minor and still keep to one of the recognized diatonic modes, and one, moreover, with which he is familiar. But this he could not do in any other mode. I have but little doubt but that this is the true explanation of this exceptional inflection of the third in the mixolydian and dorian tunes.

The English country singer usually sings the *natural* seventh, especially in mixolydian airs, instead of the minor seventh of the tempered scale. This, however, does not lead to a change of mode, although it makes it impossible faithfully to reproduce a mixolydian folk tune on a modern keyed instrument.

I have also noticed a tendency on the part of some folk singers to flatten the second of the scale. If this were done as systematically as we have seen is sometimes the case with the third, the only modes in which it could be effected within the limits of the diatonic genus would be the phrygian and aeolian. For to flatten the second in major, lydian, or mixolydian modes, would produce, in each scale, an unmelodic interval; while flattening it in the dorian mode would effect a transition to a scale having four consecutive tones. I do not know of an instance of either a phrygian or aeolian folk air in which the second of the scale is thus inflected, but I should not be surprised if, some day, one were to be recovered.

This question of intonation is a very interesting one, and a very important one, too, and one which will, I hope, engage the serious attention of the collector. Subtleties of intonation can best be noted and studied on the phonograph. The attention of the collector is ordinarily occupied with other matters, many of which are at the moment of greater importance, and it is, therefore, very difficult to record with scientific accuracy delicate shades of pitch variation. Now, however, that English collectors are using the phonograph, material for the study of this particular branch of the subject is being rapidly accumulated.[1]

[1] See article by Percy Grainger in *F.S.J.* III, No. 12 (May 1908).

CHAPTER VII

RHYTHMICAL FORMS AND MELODIC FIGURES

RHYTHMICAL FORMS

THE PATTERN of the folk tune has, throughout its evolution, been dominated by the words with which at first it was probably always associated. There is a close correspondence between the structure of melody and that of language. The analogy, however, is with metrical language only, *i.e.* poetry, not prose. Musical form in its wider meaning, *i.e.* as exhibited in symphony and sonata, has been evolved independently of language forms, with which it bears no analogy. The unit of musical form, however, is the proportioned melody; and that most certainly took shape under the controlling influence of the metrical structure of the words to which it was united.

The usual stanza of poetry contains four measured lines, not necessarily of equal length, though forming a just balance; and the music to which such a stanza is set consists, normally, of four phrases, the points of division being marked off by means of cadences. Of these the middle cadence is the most important.

If we call the several phrases A, B, C, etc., then one of the commonest of folk tune formulae is A B A, which is known to musicians as 'the primitive rondo form'. The first A is often repeated, the formula then becoming A A B A. The following beautiful dorian tune is constructed on this pattern:

THE SHIP IN DISTRESS[1]

DORIAN   A

[1] *Selected Edition*, II, p. 100.

'Just as the tide is a-flowing' (*F.S.F.S.* II, No. 37)[1] is another example of the same formula. For cadential reasons, the concluding notes of the repetitions of A are often varied, as in 'Sweet Europe' (*F.S.F.S.* II, No. 46)[2] and in the well-known air 'Green Bushes':

GREEN BUSHES[3]

Another and very common pattern is A B B A. This is the design of the following air, which may be called the stock-in-trade of every English folk singer. Whenever an English peasant singer is at a loss for a tune, he is pretty certain to fall back upon 'The Banks of the Sweet Dundee':

THE BANKS OF THE SWEET DUNDEE

[1] and *English Folk-Songs for Schools*, No. 25.
[2] and *English Folk-Songs for Schools*, No. 22.
[3] *Selected Edition*, I, p. 58.

The second B is often a free rendering of the first, rather than an exact reproduction of it, as in the above example. This formula, A B B A, is sometimes said to be peculiar to Celtic folk airs, and there are, no doubt, a large number of Irish and Scottish folk melodies that are constructed on this pattern. But the formula is quite a common one with English folk airs, and it is not entirely unknown in the folk music of other countries.

A B A C is another pattern upon which a large number of English folk tunes are constructed. C is sometimes formed out of material taken from A or B, as in 'Bruton Town' (see p. 31). On the other hand in 'Down in the Groves' (see p. 88) the last phrase is a new one. This is the case, too, in 'The Sweet Primeroses':

THE SWEET PRIMEROSES

Great economy is sometimes exhibited in the use of material by the employment of the same phrase three times in succession. A A A B is the formula of the two following airs:

LITTLE SIR HUGH[1]

1 *Selected Edition*, I, p. 22 and *Folk-Songs for Schools*, No. 1266.

THE TRUE LOVER'S FAREWELL[1]

In the last example, the double length of the last phrase balances the threefold iteration of the opening phrase.

One of the most remarkable instances of beauty achieved by the very simplest means is exemplified in the following air, the formula of which is A A B A. Its simplicity is shown not only in its melodic formula, but in the fact that it is constructed practically out of the first five notes of the scale for the sixth note is only once touched.

THE KEYS OF CANTERBURY[2]

Another instance of naive simplicity is shown in the following melody, the first phrase of which consists of two consecutive notes sounded four times in succession:

MOWING THE BARLEY[3]

1 *Selected Edition*, I, p. 92.
2 *Selected Edition*, II, p. 110 and *Folk-Songs for Schools*, No. 957 (Set 1).
3 *Selected Edition*, I, p. 102 and *English Folk-Songs for Schools*, p. 108.

The frequent iteration of one short phrase cannot be said to be so characteristic of the English folk tune as it undoubtedly is of the French folk air, and still more emphatically of that of modern Greece (see Ducoudray's *Mélodies Populaires de Grèce*). English examples may, however, be seen in 'The Drowned Lover', and in 'The Sheep-Shearing Song' (*F.S.F.S.* II, No. 32 and I No. 18)[1]. The latter is of the nature of an improvisation to which the frequent recurrence of certain small phrases gives coherence. The opening phrase of the song, consisting of five notes, recurs no less than five times in the course of the melody.

Nevertheless, this economy of invention is by no means a common habit with the makers of English folk tunes. They will more frequently squander their ideas than husband them, as for instance, in those tunes in which every phrase is a fresh one. In such cases, reliance is placed upon regularity of rhythm, and upon a certain subtle emotional connection between the several phrases, to produce the necessary feeling of coherence and unity. The two following airs are excellent examples of the formula A B C D:

A FARMER'S SON SO SWEET[2]

AS I WALKED THROUGH THE MEADOWS[3]

Second version

[1] Also *Selected Edition*, II, p. 44 and I, p. 52.
[2] *Folk-Songs for Schools*, No. 954 (Set I).
[3] *Selected Edition*, I, p. 86 and *Folk-Songs for Schools*, No. 950 (Set I).

In some folk tunes the monotony of a regular rhythm is relieved by the interpolation of an extra phrase. This added phrase often comes at the conclusion of the tune, as though it were an after-thought, as in the following, the formula of which is A B C:

EARL RICHARD[1]

The same peculiarity may be seen in 'Poor Old Horse' (*F.S.F.S.* I, No. 27).[2]

The interpolated phrase, will, however, occasionally be inserted between the third and fourth phrases, *i.e.* before instead of after the fourth phrase, as in the next example:

THE BANKS OF GREEN WILLOW[3]

Other similar examples will be found in 'The Seeds of Love', 'The True Lover's Farewell', and 'Greenland Fishery' (see pp. 102, 95, and 52).[4]

A phrase is sometimes curtailed owing to the disinclination of the singer to wait the prescribed number of beats on the last note. In a 4-time tune the last note of each phrase usually ends on the first beat

1 *English Folk-Songs for Schools*, p. 8.
2 and *English Folk-Songs for Schools*, p. 42.
3 *F.S.F.S.*, I, No. 14.
4 A further example has been omitted owing to some obscurity in its analysis.

of the bar, the next phrase beginning on the fourth beat of the same bar. In such cases the folk singer will often omit one of the two intervening beats. In accompanied tunes, the pause in the voice part is covered up by the instrumental accompaniment; but, in the absence of the latter, the singer becomes impatient and moves on at once. 'Cupid's Garden' is always sung in the following way:

CUPID'S GARDEN

For another instance, see 'The Farmer's Daughter' (*F.S.F.S.* II, No. 50). In 5-time tunes, the pause between the second and third phrases is nearly always robbed of one or two beats, as in the following example:

THE BOLD FISHERMAN[1]

Why this omission of the silent beats between the phrases is made in some songs and not in others is a little puzzling. The explanation may lie in a remark made by Chappell, when speaking of minstrel ballad airs. He says: 'One peculiar feature of these airs is the long

[1] *Selected Edition*, II, p. 32 and *Folk-Songs for Schools*, No. 1412.

interval between each phrase, so well calculated for recitation, and for recovering breath in the lengthy stories to which they were united.' Possibly, therefore, the customary pauses are observed in ballads of great length, *e.g.*, 'Earl Richard' (see p. 97), but omitted in songs or ballads of shorter length. I cannot think of a long ballad which supplies an exception to this rule.

Five-time is a very common measure in English folk melodies. Certain songs, *e.g.*, 'The Bold Fisherman' and 'Barbara Ellen', are always sung in 5-time by Somerset singers; very frequently 'Lord Bateman' also. In the latter song, the 5-measure may be a variation of 3-2, due to the impatience of the singer in omitting one of the beats of each of the dotted minims. The usual form of the tune is as follows:

LORD BATEMAN[1]

Second version

But by many singers it is rendered:

Third version

I have only once recorded a tune in 7-time, and that one was nor quite regular:

[1] *English Folk-Songs for Schools*, p. 24.

RIDING DOWN TO PORTSMOUTH

Neither 5-time nor 7-time is a distinct species of rhythm. Each is compounded of alternate bars, in the first case of three and two beats respectively, and in the second of three and four. In 'The Bold Fisherman' the alternation of two and three beats is constant throughout the tune; so that the secondary accent falls on the third beat of every 5-time bar. But in 'Riding down to Portsmouth' the alternation is irregular. In the first bar, for instance, it is four and three, the secondary accent falling on the fifth beat; while, in the second bar, the alternation is three and four, with the secondary accent on the fourth beat. Nevertheless, leaving the 9-4 bar out of consideration, the irregularity is methodical. That is to say, the secondary accent falls on the fifth beat in bars 1, 3 and 7; and on the fourth beat in bars 2, 4, 6, and 8.

A change from simple to compound time in the course of a tune is often used with very beautiful effect in English folk music, as in the following example:

THE UNQUIET GRAVE
Third version

Many folk tunes, owing to their irregular barring, look very complex on paper, but sound quite simple and natural when sung —such a tune, for example, as the following:

THE UNQUIET GRAVE

Fourth version

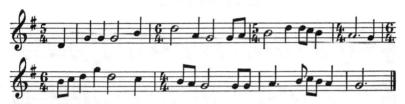

The irregularities in this air are the natural and inevitable characteristics of music that is the product of instinct. The inclination of the theorist is to reduce everything to a system, hedged round with rules as fixed and unalterable as the laws of the Medes and Persians. 'Exceptions' are the darts which lacerate the soul of the academic. Consequently, the freedom of the artist is often, and quite unnecessarily, 'cabin'd, cribb'd, and confined'. That the latter-day musician is fully alive to this is shown by the frequent occurrence of irregular barring in modern music.

It would, perhaps, be impossible to cite any particular melodic formula as especially characteristic of the English folk tune. Those that have been mentioned in this chapter—as well as many others that have had, perforce, to be omitted—are all to be found in the folk music of other countries. It may, perhaps, be said that tunes in 5-time, and irregular tunes like 'The Unquiet Grave' (see above) are found more frequently in England than in other Western European countries. But this may be only because English folk tunes, owing to their collection in more recent times, have been taken down with great care, and have consequently suffered but little from editings and 'improvements'.[1]

There is, however, one quality which is very characteristic of the

---

[1] The same would now be true of many other countries in which the collection of folk-song is still being carried on; and it cannot be said that 5-time or irregular rhythm is peculiar to the folk songs of England.

English folk melody. A large number of our folk tunes are remarkable for their large compass, the unexpectedness and width of their
intervals, and the boldness and vigour of their melodic curves.
These characteristics are exhibited in a very remarkable manner in
the following tune:

THE BROKEN TOKEN

The compass of each of the four phrases of this tune is unusually
large; the last two phrases each cover a tenth.

The interval of the octave is a common one in the folk airs of all
countries. It is often found in English folk tunes as, for example, in
the following:

THE SEEDS OF LOVE[1]

MELODIC FIGURES

There are certain melodic figures which occur very frequently
in English folk song. There is, for instance, the phrase

which is the beginning of the well-known air 'The Maid of

---

[1] *Selected Edition*, I, p. 42 and *English Folk Songs for Schools*, p. 36.

Islington'. For an example in the Aeolian mode, see 'The Wraggle Taggle Gipsies, O!' (*F.S.F.S.* I, No. 9).[1]

Another favourite beginning is

The first phrase of 'The Green Bushes' begins, for instance, in this way.

One of the phrases of a tune, generally the third, will often end with the following figure:

even when the rest of the tune is major and not mixolydian. Examples of this may be seen in 'Sovay, Sovay' (*F.S.F.S.* II, No. 31), in 'The Seeds of Love' (*F.S.J.* II, p. 24, 4th version), and elsewhere.

Sir Hubert Parry (*Art of Music*, p. 79) points out that 'a pathetic rise up to the minor seventh of the scale through the fifth' is characteristic of old German folk tunes. It is, however, equally characteristic of English folk airs. The opening phrase of 'The Ploughboy's Courtship' (*F.S.J.* II, p. 11) is as follows:

MIXOLYDIAN

and the corresponding phrase in 'The Grand Conversation of Napoleon' (*F.S.J.* II, p. 188) begins in similar manner:

Noted by Dr Vaughan Williams

MIXOLYDIAN

[1] and *Selected Edition*, I, p. 13.

E

Other examples are to be seen in 'I'm Seventeen come Sunday', (*F.S.J.* II, p. 9), and in the two middle phrases of 'Young Henry the Poacher' (*F.S.J.* II, p. 166). See also the first phrase of 'Lamentations' (p. 87) for a French example.

Another common melodic figure in English folk song is an ascending scale passage of four quavers, or semiquavers, connecting tonic and dominant, often used in the opening phrase of a melody. 'The Bold Robber' (*F.S.J.* II, p. 165) is a good example of this:

Noted by Dr Vaughan Williams

AEOLIAN

See also 'The Crystal Spring' (p. 82), where the phrase is repeated in ascending sequence; and 'William and Phyllis' (*F.S.J.* II, p. 216), where it occurs in every one of the four phrases of the melody. 'The Ploughboy's Courtship' (see above), and 'The Old Woman and the Pedlar' (*English Folk-Songs for Schools*, No. 45), are other examples.

The manner in which passing notes are used in folk music differs materially from that to which we are accustomed in modern harmonic music; and this gives rise to several very characteristic melodic figures.

The first, fourth, fifth, and eighth notes were the fixed points in the primitive scale, and are still the more stable notes in the scale of the folk singer. The position of the intermediate notes between the tonic and the subdominant, and between the dominant and tonic above, are still to some extent vague and undefined sounds in the mind of the average folk singer. Consequently, when he is proceeding downwards, say from subdominant to tonic, and wishes to connect the two notes with a single intervening sound, he will almost invariably choose the note nearest to the one which he is singing, and which, therefore, he has clearest in his mind—*i.e.* the upper one, thus:

Harmonic usage, on the other hand, would dictate

If, however, he were proceeding in the reverse direction, he would, acting on the same principle, use the lower of the two intermediate notes for his passing note, thus:

as the cultivated musician, guided by harmonic considerations, would elect.

This peculiar use of the passing note imparts to folk music a very distinctive character; for in art music it is very unusual to quit a passing note by a leap. These non-harmonic passing notes occur in a very large number of folk tunes. In the following air they are used no less than seven times:

GLENCOE

Noted by Dr Vaughan Williams

AEOLIAN

See also the seventh bar of 'Sweet Kitty', first version (p. 76) where a descending sixth is divided in this manner—

Many folk tunes, especially those of Celtic nations, begin with
the notes

These three notes form the customary intonation of the Gregorian psalm-tone.

We have already remarked that in modal melodies the seventh
note is used with much greater freedom than the leading note,
which is its analogue in the modern scale. It is hampered by no
especial restrictions and, moreover, it makes a perfect fifth with the
subdominant above it. The leading note, on the other hand, is regarded and treated as an exceptional note in the modern scale; and
it makes a diminished fifth, of course, with the subdominant above.
The seventh, second, and fourth notes of the scale, used con-
secutively, are frequently met with in modal melodies. In the next
example they occur three times:

ROBIN HOOD AND THE PEDLAR

Noted by Dr Vaughan Williams

For other examples, the reader is referred to 'Bruton Town',
'High Germany' (see pp. 31 and 73), 'Lincolnshire Farmer', 'The
Jolly Thresherman', 'Sheffield Apprentice' (*F.S.J.* II, pp. 174, 198,
169); and to the following in *F.S.F.S.*, Nos. 30, 29, 34, 78,[1] 40,[2] 48
and 67.

---

[1] and *Selected Edition*, I, pp. 1, 104, 58, II, p. 56.
[2] and *Folk Songs for Schools*, No. 1077 (Set 5).

The following metrical formulae are, perhaps, especially characteristic of the English folk tune:

etc.

etc.

Of the former, 'Lord Bateman', 'Robin Hood and the Tanner' (pp. 28–30), and 'Early, Early' (*F.S.F.S.* III, No. 70) are typical specimens; and of the latter, 'Bruton Town', 'The Ship in Distress' (pp. 31 and 92), 'Waly Waly' and 'The Bold Lieutenant' (*F.S.F.S.* III, Nos. 66[1] and 56).

In this and the preceding chapter an attempt has been made to call attention to certain technical attributes of folk music which are demonstrably of folk origin and by means of which the musical creations of the common people may to some extent be distinguished from the inventions of professed musicians. It is not pretended, for one moment, that this technical analysis has been an exhaustive one, or that a definite and conclusive result has been reached. Even if our enquiry had been more thorough and searching than the scope and purpose of this book permitted, it would, nevertheless, have failed in deducing any set of rules which would enable the critic to discriminate, without possibility of error, between folk music and composed music. A precise and scientific definition of the difference between folk and art music is, in the nature of things, unattainable. Certain technical qualities may be pointed out as peculiarly characteristic of folk music, and that we have endeavoured to do here. Yet it would be possible to produce a folk air in which not one of these qualities was present.

This is not to say, however, that our investigation has necessarily been mere waste of time. We have arrived, I venture to think, at

[1] and *Selected Edition*, I, p. 56.

certain conclusions about English folk song which, so far as they go, are not altogether valueless. Let us summarize them:

(1) A folk song is always anonymous. (This does not mean that all music that is anonymous is folk music. Anonymity is a condition, not a cause.)

(2) Modal melodies set to secular words[1] are nearly always of folk origin.

(3) Song tunes in the minor scale are either composed tunes, or folk airs that have suffered corruption.

(4) Folk tunes do not modulate (see p. 85).

(5) Folk melodies are usually non-harmonic; that is to say, they have been fashioned by those in whom the harmonic sense is undeveloped. This is shown:

(a) In the use of non-harmonic passing notes (see pp. 104–106).

(b) In a certain vagueness of tonality, especially in the opening phrases of modal tunes.

(c) In the use of the flattened seventh, after the manner of a leading note, in the final cadences of modal airs.

(6) Folk melodies often contain bars of irregular length.

(7) Prevalence of five and seven time-measures in folk airs.[1]

---

[1] These attributes are now to be found in music other than folk music to a greater extent than in Sharp's day.

CHAPTER VIII

FOLK POETRY

THIS BOOK is concerned with the music of the folk song rather than with its text. Much has been written about folk poetry in general, but very little about the traditional poetry of England.[1] It is hoped that a book on this branch of the subject will some day be written, in which scientific use will be made of the material now being amassed by collectors. No attempt is here made to forestall any such enterprise. The following observations represent no more than a brief summary of a large subject, to which are added a few general remarks concerning the character of the words of the English folk song of the present day.

Early folk poetry consisted chiefly of *ballads*, that is, poems that are narrative in substance and lyrical in form. The *song*, which is largely personal and subjective, belongs to a later development. To childhood, as to primitive man, incident and drama are ever more attractive than the analysis of feeling. The English folk singer of the present day sings both ballads and songs, but far more of the latter than of the former.

The primitive folk ballad was the literary product of an unlettered people; just as the folk tune was the musical output of the unskilled musician. It was addressed to the ear, not to the eye. It was

---

[1] For a century or so after the publication of Bishop Percy's *Reliques* (1765), interest in English and Anglo-Scottish song—chiefly balladry—was focussed on the texts to the neglect of the music (see pp. xxii–xxiii). This attitude was changed by Sharp and his contemporaries and their immediate predecessors, who, although they by no means ignored the words of the songs, regarded the collection and study of the tunes as of paramount importance. Recently in England there has been a revival of interest in the texts. This is, no doubt in part due to the work of James Reeves, himself a poet, who in *The Idiom of the People* (Heinemann, 1958) published 115 sets of words and some fragments from Cecil Sharp's unpublished manuscripts. This publication was followed by *The Everlasting Circle* (Heinemann, 1960), verse from the manuscripts of S. Baring-Gould, H. E. D. Hammond and George B. Gardiner. In America the Child-Kittredge tradition of the study of texts has been upheld and it is perhaps significant that in the majority of American universities the study of folk song lies in the domain of the Department of English.

composed in the head, and it lived in the minds and memories of those who recited it for generations before it was committed to paper. What has already been said with regard to the origin and evolution of the folk tune applies, *mutatis mutandis*, to the genesis of the folk ballad. The latter is an evolved and communal product, and is the expression of the ideas, and the reflection of the taste and feelings, not of the individual, but of the community at large.

The subjects of many of the folk ballads that are sung in different parts of Europe are substantially the same. Some of them have been traced to an Eastern origin, and they all appear to have been drawn from a common storehouse, the heritage, presumably, of the Aryan race. Folk ballads are, in many cases, only versified forms of the *Märchen* or popular tales which are found all over the world, and in countries, be it noted, that possess no literature and no professional poets, singers or reciters. The *Gesta Romanorum*, the first published collection of European folk tales, is believed to have been compiled as early as the thirteenth century, and possibly in England. It contains several stories that have passed into ballads, some of which are still being sung by the English peasantry.

Although ballad themes are thus common property, their treatment by the several nations of Europe varies very considerably. The extent and character of these variations may be studied with profit in the late Professor Child's *English and Scottish Popular Ballads*, where many of the ballads which have in recent years been collected in Great Britain may be seen and compared with their European analogues. Indeed, as Mr Andrew Lang has remarked: 'It is unnecessary to indicate more than one authority on the subject of ballads. Professor Child of Harvard . . . has collected all known ballads, with all accessible variants, and has illustrated them with an extraordinary wealth of knowledge of many literatures.'

In the evolution of the ballad the minstrel, that is, the professional singer, played no insignificant part. The ballads themselves, or at any rate many of them, originated among the common people, with whom they were current for centuries before the minstrel appropriated them and sang them. At first, the minstrel addressed himself, not to the vulgar, but to the great and noble; and these his patrons demanded something less ephemeral and limited in scope than the ballads of the people. The minstrel met this demand by presenting to his audience long Romances or Epics, which he constructed by piecing together several of the small folk ballads.

Thus, for a while, the earlier and popular ballad lost its independent existence and became merged in the longer and more complex Epic. The *Iliad* of Homer was nothing more than a concretion of a large mass of earlier Greek traditional and popular poetry; while the Norse Sagas and Eddas were composed of the older legendary and mythical ballads of Scandinavia. The *Niebelungenlied* of Germany, the *Cid* Romances of Spain, and our own Arthurian cycle all originated in like manner.

When, however, with the invention of printing, the educated classes were provided with a literature of their own, they were no longer solely dependent upon the minstrel for their amusement. The latter found his audience dwindling away, and with it his occupation, and this compelled him to turn to the common people and to cater for their tastes. The folk demanded, as they had always done, the short and concise story; something better adapted to their understanding than the involved and lengthy stories of the Romances. The minstrel met this demand by breaking up the Romances into smaller pieces, each of which formed a complete story and was within the comprehension of the multitude. So the Epics, which, in the first instance, had been built up out of the people's ballads, were now disintegrated and served up in fragments for the benefit of the people.

It would not be true to say that all our ballads have come down to us in this way. Many, no doubt, escaped absorption into the Romance and have been handed down to us from very early times without break of continuity; while others have reached us from foreign sources—for the minstrels were inveterate wanderers. Nevertheless, most authorities agree that our ballad literature consists for the most part of ballads, not of the earlier epoch—the ninth or tenth centuries—but of the second and later period, *i.e.* the fifteenth or sixteenth centuries.

The wide distribution of the ballad is illustrated by the fact that the recent investigations of collectors in England have brought to light many ballads which hitherto had been accounted exclusively Scottish. In Somerset alone I have found quite a large number of so-called Scottish ballads, *e.g.*, 'Bonnie Annie', 'Henry Martin', 'Geordie', 'Johnnie Faa', 'Earl Richard', 'The Outlandish Knights', 'John Barleycorn', 'The Crabfish', 'Lord Lovell', 'Lady Maisry', 'Lord Thomas of Winesberrie', 'Waly, Waly', and 'O, my luve's like a red, red rose'.

It may be that Scottish collectors will some day revenge themselves by proving that many of our recently discovered English ballads are no more English than Scottish. Their claim to be accounted of English origin rests, at present, upon no surer evidence than priority of collection, and this, as in the case of the Scottish ballad, may some day prove to be unsound.

The fact is that, so far as traditional poetry is concerned, England and the Lowlands of Scotland must be regarded as one area. Mr Jacobs has reached this conclusion with respect to the folk tale. In his *English Fairy Tales* (p. 231), he says:

> There is no evidence of a distinct story store of Lowland Scots differing from that of Northern or even Southern Englishmen. . . . My principle of selection has been linguistic rather than ethnographic. I accordingly distinguish two areas in which the folk-tale has passed from mouth to mouth owing to the continuity of language. The first of these includes England and runs up to the Highland line in Scotland. I made no distinction between Lowland Scotch folk-tales, when they existed, and other Northern English tales.

Motherwell writes in similar strain:

> The ballad poetry of England and Scotland has been at one time so much alike, that it is difficult, if not impossible, to discriminate between what may be considered as the native production of the one or the other. To lay down any general law for ascertaining their respective rights of property in literature of this description, is therefore impracticable.

Owing to their traditionary and communal origin the words of the folk ballad have, like its music, characteristics of their own, by means of which they may be distinguished from the 'composed' ballad of literature.

They are almost always impersonal and objective; the personal note is rarely sounded. The *dramatis personae* often speak as in a play, unannounced. The language used by the folk ballad maker is singularly simple, direct and unlaboured. Poetical figures and imagery are but rarely employed. What is superfluous is rigorously excluded; the narrator plunges into his story without preliminaries.

Economy of invention is another marked characteristic of the ballad maker. It is exhibited in the use of the same words and expressions in the description of similar incidents which by chance recur in different ballads. A question is usually answered as nearly as possible in the same words as those in which it was asked; just as a message is delivered word for word as the messenger received it. Redundancy of expression, or monotony of repetition, has no fears for the ballad singer. Indeed, the possession of certain well-worn phrases and stanzas serve to relieve the strain upon the memory of the reciter; while their popularity with the audience would not suffer by reason of their familiarity. The uneducated are like children and eagerly welcome what they have heard before. Novelty has no particular charm for them.

The hackneyed phrase is frequently to be found at the beginning and at the end of a ballad. Peasants, like all simple people, find an especial difficulty both in making a start and in consummating a conclusion. For this reason, conventional beginnings and endings are particularly helpful to them. Thus, the letter of the schoolboy will usually begin with 'I hope you are quite well', while the infant story-teller will commence with 'Once upon a time', and end with 'and they lived happily ever afterwards'. In like manner, countless ballads and songs will open with the line, 'As I went out one May morning', a fact that, by-the-way, provides the collector with a ready means of jogging a singer's memory. Times without number I have asked a singer, whose memory was exhausted, whether he had ever heard of a song beginning 'As I went out, etc.'? The question always produces a flash of recognition and very often, too, a ballad which, except for the conventional beginning, is a fresh one. The ruse rarely fails. There are other phrases which may be used in the same way. A tragic ballad that leads to the death of the hero and his spouse is usually rounded off with the well-known verses about the 'red rose' and the 'sweet briar'. What is generally known as the 'vow' verse, beginning

> There's not a swaithe goes round my waist,
> Nor a comb goes through my hair

is common to many ballads; as is also the couplet,

> Come, saddle to me my milk-white steed,
> Come, saddle me my pony too.

The method of narration, too, is a characteristic feature of the traditional ballad, which calls for notice. Much is left to the imagination of the listener; the story is sketched in a few bold strokes, with, here and there, a minute and elaborate description of some minor incident. This is one of the arts by which the ballad-maker imparts to his story a vivid sense of reality. 'Yes, Sir, and it is true', is the reply that has often been made to me by a folk singer at the conclusion of a long ballad which I have praised. Here, again, the peasant singer is like the child, and loves to think that the story which has moved him is not fictitious but true. To him there is no tale like the true tale; and, to heighten the sense of reality, he will often lay the scene of his story in his own locality. I have even heard 'Torquay' substituted for 'Turkey' in the ballad of 'Lord Bateman' —though this may admit of another explanation.

There is no feature that is more characteristic of the popular ballad than the refrain. It forms almost the invariable adjunct to the ballad that has any claim to antiquity.

There is reason to believe that the primitive ballad was not only communal in authorship but communal in performance also, and that it was danced as well as sung.[1] As time went on, dance and song

---

[1] The origin of the ballad and its connection with the dance, which its etymology suggests, are controversial matters. In the Faroe Islands chain-dances accompany the singing of ballads, and some see in this a relic of the medieval carole. Whether or not the ballad was originally associated with the dance, the accompanying tunes often have a dance-like quality. This wedding of a tragic text to a gay tune does not have the incongruous effect that might be imagined, but, on the contrary, it seems to heighten the dramatic tension.

became divorced, each taking on a separate and independent existence, and developing along its own lines. With this separation the words 'ballet' and 'ballad' became differentiated, the former being applied to the dance only, and the latter to the song. Curiously, the synonymous use of these two words still survives. The English peasant will often say that he has learned a particular song 'off a *ballet*', meaning thereby a 'ballad-sheet'; or, 'Never had no ballet to it'—as a singer once said to me.

Very soon after the separation of the song and dance had taken place, the former became less communal in its performance. A 'leader' of the ballad made his appearance, between whom and the crowd the performance was apportioned. As time went on, the part allotted to the multitude, which at first was of considerable importance, gradually diminished until it had dwindled down to the chanting of certain stereotyped phrases at regular intervals, the whole of the narrative portion being supported by the leader. Hence the solo and chorus—or refrain—with which we are all familiar. Nowadays, the crowd has been dispossessed altogether, and both narrative and chorus are sung by the soloist. When the refrain was sung by the people it served the dual purpose of providing the minstrel with breathing space—a very necessary thing when we remember the length of some of the ancient ballads—and of giving him time to recall his next lines or, maybe, of inventing them when he was improvising.

This popular method of performance, *viz.*, solo and refrain, was imported into the Church very early in its history, where it laid the foundations of antiphonal singing.

Mr Burgess, in his *Plainsong and Gregorian Music* (pp. 23-4), says:

> The most popular method in the Western Church, and, probably the only one used during the first four centuries, was that known as Responsorial chanting. The psalm was chanted by one voice, the people responding after each verse with an unvarying refrain often taken from the psalm itself. It was probably from this germ that the whole system of Antiphons developed. The Antiphonal singing mentioned by ancient writers probably consisted in a similar

arrangement—one body of voices singing the psalm, another set of singers responding with the refrain, or Antiphon, after each verse. (See p. 79.)

The ballad refrain was not, so far as is known, taken from the ballad itself, as the antiphon appears to have been taken from the psalm. But many authorities assert that the song refrains were fragments of still older ballads, cunningly chosen by the minstrel to create a suitable atmosphere. The refrains of many Danish ballads have been so traced, and it is well known that the old French poets often incorporated lines of ancient songs in the refrains of their own poems.

The ancient refrain takes several forms. It may alternate between every line of the ballad, thus converting a couplet into a four-lined stanza, as in 'The Coasts of Barbary':

> There were two ships from England set·sails,
> *Blow high! blow low! and so sailed we.*
> The King of Prussia and the Prince of Wales,
> *Cruising down the coasts of Barbary.*

Or, it may take the form of a stanza as long as, or even longer than, the verses, between which it is interpolated, as in 'The Two Magicians' (*F.S.F.S.* I, No. 19).[1] Or again, it may consist of a single line attached to the end of every verse, as in 'Earl Richard' (*F.S.F.S.* No. 28);[2]

> There was a little shepherd maid
> Kept sheep one summer day:
> And by there came a fair young man,
> Who stole her heart away.
> *Line, twine, the willow and the dee.*

The form of the refrain of 'The coasts of Barbary' is probably the most ancient of the three types; the lines make sense, and are in keeping with the subject of the ballad. Irrelevant words marked a later period, and one of decadence, such as, for instance:

[1] and *Selected Edition*, II, p. 8.
[2] and *English Folk-Songs for Schools*, No. 4.

> Say can you make me a cambric shirt
> *Sing ivy leaf, sweet william and thyme,*
> Without any needle or needle work?
> And you shall be a true lover of mine.

The third stage was reached when, with the loss of meaning, the words themselves became corrupted into the meaningless jingles with which we are all familiar. This process of decline may be traced in the refrain of 'The Lover's Tasks', which has been taken down in the following forms:

(1). Parsley, sage, rosemary and thyme.
(2). Sing ivy leaf, sweet william and thyme.
(3). Every rose grows merry in thyme.
(4). Sober and grave grows merry in time.
(5). Whilst every grove rings with a merry antine.

The last four are probably corruptions of the first.

How easily words will become corrupt when they convey no meaning to the singer is illustrated by the following incident. I once noted a set of words of 'Little Sir Hugh' (*F.S.F.S.* III, No. 68)[1] from a very bright and intelligent singer. Her version of the ballad was a very full one and quite intelligible, except for the two opening lines which she sang as follows:

> Do rain, do rain, American corn,
> Do rain both great and small.

The singer was quite unable to explain these astounding lines, but on comparing them with other recorded versions of the same ballad I discovered that they were but a corruption of,

> It do rain, it do rain in merry Lincoln,
> It do rain both great and small.

To Somerset singers Lincoln is an unknown name, and the

---

[1] and *Selected Edition*, I, p. 22.

presence of this single and unintelligible word was enough to corrupt the meaning of the whole passage.

Occasionally, a jingling refrain may be traced to a foreign tongue *e.g.*, 'Hey, Derry Down!', whicn is said to have been the Welsh burden of an old Druid song, signifying 'Let us hie to the Green Oak'. It would be as well, perhaps, not to attach too much credence to suggested explanations of this kind, which must be highly speculative. Nevertheless, we may, I think, take it that the jingling refrain is a corruption of words that were not, in their origin, meaningless. Such a refrain as

To my oor, bag boor, bag nigger, bag waller and ban-ta-ba-loo!

is so extraordinary that it is impossible to believe it to be a mere collocation of arbitrarily chosen syllables. Whatever its origin, the jingle is often very beautiful in itself as mere sound, and, moreover, it provides the folk singers with an excuse for some delightful strains of pure melody.

Although the preceding observations apply for the most part to the ballad, some of them are equally applicable to the song. The impersonal note is, perhaps, the most distinctive attribute of the ballad. The song is more subjective. If less romantic and imaginative than the ballad, it is in closer relationship with the life and present interests of the singer. In point of time the song succeeded the ballad, of which, in a sense, it is the lineal descendant.

'Love' is the perennial theme of the folk singer of all lands. The English peasant is no exception to this rule, and a very large proportion of his songs are love songs. These are not, however, of the intense, erotic type, which is so common among the Southern nations of Europe. The Englishman's love song is of the adventurous, open-air order, with love at first sight, hastily reciprocated, to the accompaniment of nightingales and the breaking into blossom of buds at Spring time. 'As I went out one May morning' is the motto which might be affixed to the majority of them. It is the Englishman's way to look on the bright side of things, to view life from the standpoint of May rather than of December. The lovers are milk-maidens and ploughboys, or, very often, as in the fairy tale, of different stations in life; the Squire is enamoured with the milk-maid, or the Squire's daughter with the ploughboy or sailor. Usually the course of true love runs smoothly enough, and it is only a small proportion of English love songs that end unhappily, and still fewer that lead to disaster. And even then, the jilted one is not driven to despair; she will console herself in the last verse with the comforting reflection that—

> There's many a dark and cloudy morning
> Turns out to be a sunshiny day.

or accept the position with fortitude and remark:

> And I shall not die for my love
> Young man believe me.

The picture of the disconsolate lover bemoaning his fate and meditating suicide is not by any means unknown to English folk song, but it is far less common than in the folk literature of many other nations.

Another theme favoured by the English folk singer is that of the rover or wanderer. 'I am a rover', or 'roving is my trade', are expressions that constantly recur in English folk ditties. This is remarkable when we remember that the peasant usually spends his life in the village of his birth, from whence he will rarely adventure beyond a circle of a few miles' radius. The love of travel and adventure is his, nevertheless, and it is, probably, just because circumstances bar him from indulging his desires that he gives rein to this particular fancy in his songs. He is never tired of singing of the navvy-man, the travelling tinker, or the recruiting serjeant, and those whose occupations lead to wandering.

On the other hand, the actual occupations of his life less often form the subject of the peasant's song, although there are a certain number in which the pleasures of ploughing, sowing, reaping and other farming operations are extolled. In days gone by, songs of this type were, perhaps, more numerous, but, with the passing of the harvest home and the village feast, many of them have disappeared. After all, it is not unnatural, seeing that his hours of work are long and arduous, that the labourer should find more recreation in songs of romance and adventure than in those which remind him of his toil.

For a like reason, the sailor, who is an inveterate songster, revels in romantic love songs and ballads of adventure. It is only in the drawing-room or on the stage that he sings of 'Ho! Heave Ho!'. The chantey is, however, an exception. That is, of course, a genuine sailor song, the direct outcome of the peculiar conditions appertaining to life on board ship. The chantey is sung by sailors only when they are actually engaged upon their work, and for the purpose of lightening it. It is, however, the exclusive possession of the sailor. The peasant would never sing a chantey any more than a sailor would sing a sheep-shearing song. But, on ordinary occasions, that is when he is singing for amusement, the sailor sings precisely the same songs as the country people, except that he shows a partiality for those ballads in which the hero is a sailor, or in which the scene of the adventures is laid at sea. It is such ditties as these which are ordinarily known as 'sea-songs'; but they are sung just as frequently by the country folk, who have never seen the sea, as by those who have spent the greater part of their lives upon it. The only song of this type that I have never heard in the country districts is that very beautiful ballad 'Spanish Ladies'; but that, I believe, is, properly speaking, a capstan chantey.

What is generally accepted as the patriotic song is conspicuous by its absence from the repertoire of the folk singer. Such songs as 'Heart of Oak', 'Rule, Britannia!' etc. are of course not folk songs; nor are they sung by the folk. When wars are mentioned they are but the minor incidents in the course of an adventurous love song, as in 'Polly Oliver' or 'High Germany', where the heroine dresses up in the garb of a soldier that she may accompany her lover to the battlefield. The English folk singer has, however, his heroes, and he will sing of Nelson, or Napoleon, or General Wolfe. But the outlaw and the freebooter appeal to his imagination with greater force than the successful military or naval commander. Robin Hood, Dick Turpin or Henry Martin are his real heroes.

The subjects of English folk song are rarely drawn from history or politics. I have never happed upon a folk song in Somerset which contained an allusion to the battle of Sedgemoor, or to any of the disturbances which took place in the county during the great revolution. The only historical ballad I have recovered in the West is one in which the death of Lady Jane Seymour, in giving birth to Edward the Sixth, is recorded. And this is probably because Lady Jane came of a Somerset family, and is said to have been born near Bridgwater. It is generally assumed that the subjects of many of the more ancient ballads were founded upon historical events, but the attempts that have been made to confirm this, chiefly by Scottish commentators, are not very encouraging.

In some cases, no doubt, the ballad story did really originate in some actual historical event. More often, however, the latter is what is technically known as an 'intrusion'. An incident occurs in real life similar to that narrated in a ballad, with which it is for ever afterwards associated. To increase the likeness, and that it may conform more closely with the details of the actual occurrence, the ballad is gradually and insensibly modified. Names of persons and places are changed, dates are altered, and so forth, and it is upon these that, in after days, misleading and unwarranted conclusions are often based.

The words of 'The Seeds of Love', for instance, are usually associated with a Mrs Habergam, of Whalley in Lancashire, simply because the story of her life, which was no doubt well known in her neighbourhood, corresponded more or less with the incidents narrated in the song. Naturally enough, a popular belief soon grew up in Lancashire that Mrs Habergam had herself composed the words of the song; and this is the explanation that is often accepted. There is, however, little doubt that 'The Seeds of Love' is a modern variant of an older ballad, 'The Sprig of Thyme', modified, in the way above explained, to suit the case of Mrs Habergam.

Songs in praise of sport and hunting are not, apparently, held in high estimation by the folk. 'When bucks a-hunting go' is probably one of the best, as it is also one of the best known songs of this class. The hunting songs that are usually sung in the country districts are either very poor folk songs, or not folk songs at all. The majority of them are the productions of eighteenth-century musicians, and they are more often sung by farmers than by peasants. The illegitimate form of sport, *i.e.*, poaching, is a subject which possesses far greater attractiveness to the folk singer. Those poaching songs, too, that end with hangings, or transportations to Botany Bay, are especially popular.

Drinking songs, too, are scarcely ever to be found in the repertoire of the folk singer. Incidental allusions to drink are common enough, but the thorough-going bacchanalian song, of the type of 'Down among the dead men', is unknown to the folk singer—so far as my experience goes. The only drinking song I have ever heard in the country is 'Fathom the Bowl', and that is probably not a folk song.

'Execution' songs, which recount the adventures and subsequent hangings of notorious criminals, possess a strange fascination for the peasant singer, partly because many of them are of local origin, but mainly, perhaps, because they purport to be true. They are valuable to the collector, not on account of their words, which are modern doggerel as a rule, but because of their tunes, which are often fine old ballad airs. A tune that is often used for this purpose is 'Come all ye faithful Christians' (see p. 35). With regard, however, to the poverty of the words of the 'execution' song, exception must be made for 'The Berkshire Tragedy', which is a fine old ballad and stands in a category of its own.

Ballads which deal with the supernatural or the marvellous are not often met with nowadays, and those that are still to be heard have usually suffered grievously at the hands of latter-day editors by whom the supernatural element has been either eliminated, or rationalized into conformity with the more material beliefs of the present day. 'The Unquiet Grave' is, happily, an exception to this rule. There is no more popular song to be heard in the countryside; it is freely sung by the old singers, and, probably, in very much

the same form as that in which it has been sung for centuries. 'The
Shooting of his Dear', 'Little Sir Hugh' (*F.S.F.S.* I, No. 16 and III
No. 68)[1] and 'The Cruel Ship's Carpenter' and other examples of
the same class.

Songs in praise of the home and of the virtues of domesticity are
not to be found amongst genuine folk songs. Songs of this type are
too sentimental for the peasant taste, and are alien to the spirit of
folk song. The vision of the rustic is neither very wide nor very
narrow. On the one hand, he is not attracted by subjects of large
national interest, nor, on the other, by those which deal with his
own private and family life. The domestic virtues he may or may
not have, but he certainly does not sing about them. There is no
song more popular with country singers all over England than 'The
Wraggle Taggle Gipsies, O!', and this, probably, because it extols
the healthful, open-air pleasures of the vagrant life, as against the
enervating, smug, indoor life of the parlour.

There are, too, very few folk songs that can be classed as
humorous. When humour enters into the peasant song, and it is but
rarely, it is of the boisterous, exuberant and obvious type; it is
neither subtle nor delicate. Nothing can be further from the truth
than the popular belief that a folk song is invariably a comic song.
Those song which recount the clown-like adventures of the yokel
on his journey to London, and which were so popular in the
Vauxhall and Ranelagh days, were composed songs, written by
contemporary musicians for middle-class consumption. It is not to
be expected that the peasant would go out of his way to sing, much
less to invent, songs in which he himself was held up to ridicule.
Popular superstitions die hard, and it will be long before it is
generally realized that soldiers are not in the habit of singing
patriotic songs in the canteen; that sailors do not sing of the perils
of the sea in the fo'castle; and that peasants neither burlesque themselves in their songs, nor sing about 'Home, Sweet Home'. Peasant,
sailor and soldier, one and all prefer the love-song of romance to
anything else.

---

1 and *Selected Edition*, I, p. 22.

Cumulative songs are very popular with country singers, and they used to be in great request at harvest homes, sheep-shearings and other festive gatherings.

The cumulative song is one in which the verses increase in length, in arithmetical progression, each verse consisting of a repetition of the previous one, with the addition of one or more lines. 'The House that Jack built' is a well-known example of this type of song. 'The Twelve days of Christmas', 'The Everlasting Circle', 'The Dilly Song', 'The Barley Mow', 'One man shall mow my meadow', and 'The Mallard', are all cumulative songs, and most folk singers know one or more of them.

Cumulative songs take a long while to sing, especially those that are retrogressive as well as progressive. 'The twelve days of Christmas' is one of these. The first verse deals with the first day, the second verse with the first two days, and so on, until the whole of the twelve days are introduced in the twelfth verse. At this point the verses decrease in length; the thirteenth verse dealing with eleven days, the fourteenth verse with ten days, and so on, until the singer triumphantly reaches the twenty-third and last verse, which completes the circle, and lands him at the point from which he set out.

This is a particularly popular song with some singers, and the ability to 'go through' with it, without hesitation or mistake, is regarded as a great test of memory, and, on convivial occasions, as an absolute proof of sobriety!

To those who have never heard a cumulative song properly sung by a folk singer, the above description will probably convey a very false impression. As a matter of fact, many of them are exceedingly beautiful. The short musical phrases are combined in a varied and skilful manner in the different verses, and the song, as a whole, produces an effect that is quite delightful.

'I have a song to sing, O!' in Gilbert and Sullivan's *Yeomen of the Guard* is a modern recension of 'The Dilly Song'.

Mention must be made, too, of the carols, which in days gone by were very numerous and very popular. The traditional carol stands midway between the hymn and the ballad, and may be regarded with equal propriety as a secular hymn or as a sacred ballad. The subject of the carol is usually taken from some incident in the Christ story, narrated in the gospels, or in the legends and stories of doubtful authenticity recorded in the apocryphal gospels and elsewhere. Carols are usually associated with the festivals of Christmas and the Epiphany, but there are Easter and Ascension carols as well. Musically regarded, the traditional carol is not to be distinguished from the folk song; indeed, the broadside carol was often directed to be sung to some well-known secular and popular air. Several genuine folk carols, some of them of supreme beauty, have recently been recorded by collectors in England (see *F.S.J.* vols. I and II). But they are fast disappearing, together with the simple belief in the literal truth of the Gospel story, and that child-like attitude towards religion of which they were the faithful expression. Such carols as 'Nowell, Nowell', 'God rest you merry, gentlemen', 'The withy carol', 'The White Paternoster', etc., not only remind us of days gone by, but are present and national possessions of the highest value. In some parts of England, especially in the West, almost every hamlet had, and in some cases still has, its own carols, which were highly prized and jealously guarded from appropriation by neighbouring villages. But these, so far as my personal experience goes, were always 'composed' carols, often harmonized, and obviously the productions of seventeenth- and eighteenth-century village musicians, possessing no great musical or literary value. Like all folk products, the genuine traditional carols were not confined to any one locality, but were widely distributed.

Wassail songs, and carols associated with the May-day festival, are pagan survivals, which, although they have since been modified by contact with Christian customs, must be sharply distinguished from the carols connected with the festivals of the Church, which latter were the direct outcome of Christian belief.

Before concluding this very incomplete summary, something must needs be said about the broadside or ballet, which has had so marked and in many ways so detrimental an influence upon the words of the folk-ballad and song.[1] The ballad broadside, which sprang into life very soon after the invention of printing, consisted of a single sheet of paper, upon one side of which were printed the words only of the ballad, or song. These broadsheets were hawked about the country by packmen, who frequented fairs, village festivals, and public gatherings of all sorts, and who advertised their wares by singing them in market places, on village greens, in the streets of the towns, and wherever they could attract an audience. In this way ballads and songs were disseminated all over the land. In later days the broadside would have two or more ballads printed upon it, and sometimes several ballads were bound together and distributed in small books of three or four pages, called 'garlands'.

Many of these broadside ballads were the productions of the literary hacks of the towns, the Fleet Street scribblers of the day; occasionally they were written by ballad-mongers of literary repute, like Martin Parker. Some of them were learned by the hawkers during their country excursions, and were afterwards recited by them, for a consideration, to their employers. In this manner the traditional ballad found its way on to the broadside, but, usually, in a very garbled form, and after many editings. Consequently, the ballad sheet, while it aided the popularization of the ballad, also tended to vulgarize it. It was only very rarely that a genuine traditional ballad found its way on to a broadside without suffering corruption. A broadside version of a ballad is usually, therefore, a very indifferent one, and vastly inferior to the genuine peasant song.

With very rare exceptions, and for obvious reasons, the broadside contained the words only of the songs, not the music to which they were sung. The music of the folk song did not, therefore,

---

[1] On the other hand, credit must be given for the part that the broadside has played in the preservation of traditional song. Had it not been for its agency many songs might not have survived. And with the loss of the text, which in itself might not have been of great value, we should have suffered the loss of the tune.

For further information on the broadside ballad, the reader is referred to *The Broadside Ballad* (London, 1962) by Leslie Shepard, to *American Balladry from British Broadsides* by Malcolm Laws, Jr. (Philadephia, [1957] 1964) and to *The Common Muse*, edited by Pinto and Rodway (London, 1957).

suffer corruption through the agency of the ballad sheet, as was the case with the words. We must remember also that the folk singer would often learn modern and very indifferent sets of words from the broadside, and sing them to old tunes, after the manner of the 'execution songs' already mentioned. These, no doubt, are the chief reasons why the music of the folk song of today has been more faithfully preserved than its text. For it must be confessed that the words of the folk song often come to the collector of today in a very corrupt and incomplete state. The truth is that the twentieth-century collector is a hundred years too late. The English ballad is moribund; its account is well-nigh closed.

This conclusion corroborates that which was reached by the Society of Antiquaries of Newcastle-upon-Tyne, when, in 1855, they set about the collection of the Northumbrian ballads. In their first report they recorded that, so far as the words were concerned, they were 'half-a-century too late'.

And yet, although page after page of the collector's notebooks are filled with scraps of imperfectly-remembered broadside versions, here and there will be found, sometimes a whole ballad, more often a verse or two, or, perhaps, a phrase only of genuine folk-made poetry. It is only from scraps of this kind that an estimate can be formed, and that a speculative one, of what the English ballad was in its prime. It has been pointed out that the Scottish ballad is immeasurably finer and more poetical than the English. But the comparison is scarcely a fair one. For the songs of Lowland Scotland were collected more than a hundred years ago, when ballad singing was still a living art; whereas we in England have so neglected our opportunities that we are only now making a belated attempt to gather up the crumbs. Such ballads as 'The Unquiet Grave', which have survived in more or less incorrupt form, are there to remind us of the loss that we have suffered from the unworthy neglect of past opportunities.

Over and above this question of word corruption, there are some songs, which, for other reasons, can only be published after extensive alteration or excision. Some of these, happily only a few, are gross and coarse in sentiment and objectionable in every way. I am convinced, however, that the majority of these are individual and not communal productions, and cannot therefore be classed as genuine folk songs. At any rate, I know that they offend against the communal sense of propriety, that the verdict of the community is expressly against them, and that those who sing them do so fully understanding that they are bad, vicious and indefensible.

But there are also a large number of folk songs which transgress the accepted conventions of the present age, and which would shock the susceptibilities of those who rank reticence and reserve amongst the noblest of the virtues. These are not, strictly speaking, bad songs; they contain nothing that is really wrong or unwholesome. And they do not violate the communal sense of what is right and proper. They are sung freely and openly by peasant singers, in entire innocence of heart, and without the shadow of a thought that they contain anything that is objectionable, or that they themselves are committing any offence against propriety in singing them.

This is a phenomenon which opens up a large question. The keynote of folk poetry, as we have already shown, is simplicity and directness without subtlety—as in the Bible narratives and Shakespeare. This characteristic might be mistaken for a want of refinement by those who live in an age where subtlety and circumlocution are extensively practised. This question comes especially to the fore when the most universal and elemental of all subjects is treated, that of love and the relations of man to woman. Its very intimacy and mystery cause many minds to shrink from expressing themselves openly on the subject, as they would shrink from desecrating a shrine. The ballad maker has no such feeling. He has none of that delicacy, which, as often as not, degenerates into pruriency. Consequently, he treats 'the way of a man with a maid' simply and directly, just as he treats every other subject. Those, therefore, who would study ballad literature must realize that they will find in it none of those feelings and unuttered thoughts which are characteristic of a more self-conscious but by no means more pure-minded age. Nevertheless, however much we may admire the simplicity and the straightforward diction of the ballad-maker, we have to realize that other times and other people are not so simple-minded and downright, and that what is deemed fit and proper for one period is not necessarily so for others. The folk-song editor, therefore, has perforce to undertake the distasteful task of modifying noble and beautiful sentiments in order that they may suit the minds and conform to the conventions of another age, where such things would not be understood in the primitive, direct and healthy sense.[1]

These songs, however, in that they throw a searching light upon the character of the peasant, possess great scientific value. For this reason alone, it is obviously the duty of the collector to note them down conscientiously and accurately, and to take care that his transcriptions are placed in libraries and museums, where they may be examined by students and those who will not misunderstand them.

Songs of the type that we have been discussing, as well as those whose words are incomplete or corrupt, present a knotty problem to the collector who would publish them for popular use. Only those who have tried their hands at editing a folk song can realize the immense difficulty of the task. To be successful the editor must be in close sympathy with the aims of the folk poet. He must divest himself of all acquired literary tricks, be alert to avoid ana-chronisms, and contrive to speak in the simple and direct language of the peasant. The high estimation in which the best Scottish traditional poetry is deservedly held is due in no small measure to the genius and sympathetic insight of those who edited it. Amongst these Burns was, of course, pre-eminent. But he was a peasant as well as a poet, and represented the peasant element in song. He was,

---

[1] Times have changed. There is little in English folk song that would be taboo to the freer conventions of present-day society. As a matter of fact, the bringing to light of a few 'outspoken' verses, hitherto unpublished, has led to a false conception of the nature of the original 'unedited' words. An examination of Cecil Sharp's manuscript collection will show that of the authentic folk songs ninety per cent could be sung word for word as noted without bringing a blush to the cheek of the most decorous of maiden aunts. Apart from the small proportion of songs which might have offended the susceptibilities of a former generation on account of their forthrightness, there are a number of love songs in which use is made of a delicate and often poetic form of symbolism. This is far removed from the *double entendre* favoured by more sophisticated members of society. The subject has been treated with imagination and insight by James Reeves in Parts 5 and 6 of his Introduction to *The Everlasting Circle (op. cit.).*

moreover, an enthusiastic collector of the folk tunes of his own country, of which he possessed an intimate, if not a technical, knowledge. Yet, it cannot truthfully be said that even Burns was uniformly successful in his revisions, although in such songs as 'John Anderson, my Jo', or 'O! my luve's like a red, red rose', he approached perfection. It must be remembered, too, that he confined his attention to the songs, and that he scarcely touched the ballads, which were left to Sir Walter Scott and others to recover and to edit. Who will do for our English ballads and songs what Scott and Burns did for the Scottish?

CHAPTER IX

FOLK SINGERS AND THEIR SONGS

O NE OF the most amazing and puzzling things about the English folk song is the way in which it has hitherto escaped the notice of the educated people resident in the country districts. When I have had the good fortune to collect some especially fine songs in a village, I have often called upon the Vicar to tell him of my success. My story has usually been received, at first, with polite incredulity, and, afterwards, when I have displayed the contents of my notebook, with amazement. Naturally, the Vicar finds it difficult to realize that the old men and women of his parish, whom he has known and seen day by day for many a long year, but whom he has never suspected of any musical leanings, should all the while have possessed, secretly treasured in their old heads, songs of such remarkable interest and loveliness.

It would not be just—indeed, it would be an impertinence—to ascribe this ignorance on the part of the village priest to any lack of interest in his parishioners. For intimacy with a peasant may go a long way and yet stop short of his songs. The peasant guards these with jealous care. His songs are his own, the creations of his own class; he is proud of them; they are exceedingly precious to him; they have come to him as an inheritance, and he rates them at a high value. His instinct tells him that they are very different from the songs of educated people—which is, unhappily, only too true; has he not been entertained at Penny Readings?—and fear of ridicule makes him secretive. For a like reason he will instinctively disguise his dialect, so far as he can, when educated people speak with him. Indeed, you must be on exceedingly good terms with him if you would hear him talk in his own native tongue; and still more intimate with him before he will sing to you his own native songs.

This may be the chief reason why the leisured classes have never discovered the fact that the English folk possess music and a ballad literature of their own, and that their chief amusement and recreation for generations past has been the singing of folk songs. But it is not the only reason. The clergyman of the village is usually present at the annual Club feast, and very often at the Harvest Home, and folk singing is very much in evidence on these festive occasions. But the songs that he then hears are sung with rough voices and without accompaniment, and, thus disguised, he dismisses them as crude, archaic music, quite unworthy of his serious consideration.

The late Carl Engel, in his *Literature of National Music* (p. 32), commented upon the supposed lack of English folk music in the following terms:

> It seems rather singular that England should not possess any printed collection of its national songs with the airs as they are sung at the present day; while almost every other European nation possesses several comprehensive works of this kind. . . . Some musical enquirers have expressed the opinion that the country people in England are not in the habit of singing while at their work in the fields, or when towards evening they are returning to their homes; and that those social gatherings during the long winter evenings, in which the Germans and other Continental nations delight in singing their favourite songs, are unknown to the English rustics. However, this opinion would probably be found to be only partially correct if search were made in the proper places. . . . There are, in some of the shires, rather isolated districts, in which the exertions of a really musical collector would be not entirely resultless.

So far as I am aware these views were never challenged. No English musician felt himself called upon to test their truth or falsity. Yet Engel wrote at a period, thirty or forty years ago, when folk singing in England was a living art, and when the old singers of today were young men and women, in their prime as singers. A musician at that time could have walked into almost any country village in England and gathered without trouble a rich harvest of folk song. He did not do so because, convinced that he came of an unmusical race, there seemed to him no reason to question the assertion that his countrymen had no folk songs of their own.

I have talked with scores of old country people on this subject of folk singing. They all repeat the same tale. Everyone sang in their young days, they will tell you; they went to their work in the mornings singing; they sang in the fields, and they trudged home in the evenings to the accompaniment of song. Talk to any old peasant and you will find that he has an intimate acquaintanceship with the old songs. Maybe he will confess that he himself was 'never no zinger', but he will volunteer to 'tell' you a song, and own to the ability to join in when others are there to give him a lead. The evidence is overwhelming that, as recently as thirty or forty years ago, every country village in England was a nest of singing birds. It seems impossible to believe that this was unknown to the squires or to the clergy. We had rather conclude, I think, that they did know it, but that they failed to appreciate its significance.

The folk singers of today, as I have already remarked, are the last of a long line that stretches back into the mists of far-off days. Their children were the first of their race to reject the songs of their fore-fathers. Nowadays, the younger generations despise them, and, when they mention them, it is with a lofty and supercilious air and to pour ridicule upon them. The old singers, of course, hold the modern song in like contempt, although they accept the changed conditions with a quiet dignity, which is not without its pathos. One old singer once said to me, 'Our tunes be out o' vashion. They young volk come a-zingin' thicky comic zongs, and I don't know they, and they won't hearken to my old-vashioned zongs.' The old order changeth, and the old singers realize that their day has gone and that they and their songs are 'out 'o vashion'. Imagine, then, their joy when the collector calls upon them and tells them of his love for the old ditties. He has only to convince them of his sincerity to have them at his mercy. They will sing to him in their old quavering voices until they can sing no more; and, when he is gone, they will ransack their memories that they may give him of their best, should he, perchance, call again, as he promised.

Attention must be drawn to the conventional method of singing adopted by folk singers. During the performance the eyes are closed, the head upraised, and a rigid expression of countenance maintained until the song is finished. A short pause follows the conclusion, and then the singer relaxes his attitude and repeats in his ordinary voice the last line of the song, or its title. This is the invariable ritual on formal occasions. It does not proceed from any lack of appreciation. The English peasant is by nature a shy man and undemonstrative, and on ceremonious occasions, as when he is singing before an audience, he becomes very nervous and restrained, and welcomes the shelter afforded by convention. I have never seen women sing in this way; but then they never perform in public, and only very rarely when men are present. If you would prevail upon a married woman to sing to you, you must call upon her when her man is away at work, that is, if he be a singer himself. She will never sing to you in his presence until you have come to know both her and her husband very intimately.

A man will sing naturally enough, and without any formality, by his own fireside. I have known him on such occasions to get quite excited when he is singing a song that moves him, and to rise from his chair and gesticulate and, perhaps, beat the table to enforce the rhythm of the tune. One old woman once sang to me out in the open fields, where she was working, and between the verses of her song she seized the lapel of my coat, and looked up into my face with glistening eyes to say, 'Isn't it beautiful?'

Singers have often said to me 'When I were young I used to dance thicky zong, but I be too old now'—an interesting survival of the days before the sister arts of singing and dancing were divorced. 'The Keys of Heaven' is a song that often used to be danced and sung with dramatic action by a man and his wife.

The repertoires of many of the old singers are very extensive. I have taken down as many as a hundred genuine folk songs from a single singer, and to recover as many as thirty or even forty is no unusual experience. These figures, moreover, must be doubled to arrive at the number of songs such singers really know; for, for every song that the collector will take from them, they will know another that he does not want, either because he has already noted

it down from someone else, or because it is not a folk song. Miss
Lucy Broadwood writes of a Sussex singer, Mr Henry Burstow,
(*F.S.J.* Vol. I, p. 139): 'He is proud of knowing four hundred songs,
and keeps a valuable list of their titles, of which he allowed me to
make a copy. He once, by request, sang *all his songs* to a gentleman;
"it took a month to do it!" '

Mr Percy Merrick, another well-known collector, has published
in the *Folk-Song Journal* (Vol. I, pp. 64 and 269), fifty-seven songs,
all of which he recovered from the same singer.

The old singers were proud, too, of the large numer of songs
that they could sing. To prove their prowess they would often
arrange singing matches, which would last for several evenings.
Each night the competitors would meet and sing songs alternately,
until one of them had exhausted his repertore, when the loser paid
for his defeat in being mulcted in the cost of all the refreshments that
had been consumed during the contest. The unsuccessful com-
petitor has often told me that the day after his discomfiture several
songs came back to his mind, which, if he had remembered at the
time, might have reversed the verdict. This, I have no doubt, is
true enough; you never know when you have got to the bottom of
a singer's memory.

The quality of the voice of the average folk singer is, of course,
thin and poor, but that is because he is an old man. You cannot
expect a man of eighty years of age, or upwards, to sing with the
resonant voice of youth; the wonder is that he can sing at all. The
folk singer is, however, no mean vocalist. He is a past master in the
art of welding together words and tune, *i.e.*, in enunciating his
syllables with great clearness, while maintaining an unbroken
stream of melody. He sings, too, as a rule, with very pure intonation, except when the compass of a song is so wide that he is
driven on to the extreme notes of his voice. I have already said that
many singers take the natural seventh, especially in mixolydian
tunes, and the natural third, instead of the corresponding tempered
intervals. Folk singers have, no doubt, acquired their vocal skill
from constantly singing without accompaniment. The unevenness
of tone which mars the vocalization of all but the very best of

F

singers is directly attributable to the practice of singing habitually with instrumental accompaniment.

But, it must be remembered that the vocal method of the folk singer is inseparable from the folk song. It is a cult which has grown up side by side with the folk song, and is, no doubt, part and parcel of the same tradition. When, for instance, an old singing-man sings a modern popular song, he will sing it in quite another way. The tone of his voice will change and he will slur his intervals, after the approved manner of the street singer. Indeed, it is usually quite possible to detect a genuine folk song simply by paying attention to the way in which it is sung.

Fok singers like to sing in as high a pitch as possible, and they will often apologize for not being able, on account of age, to sing their songs high enough.[1] Sometimes this habit, especially in the case of nervous singers, will lead to the gradual raising of the pitch of a song, verse by verse, until the singer reaches the limit of his voice, when it is necessary to come to his assistance and start him afresh in a lower key. Singers, too, will often take a particular interval in a song too sharp or too flat. This, again, will result in the gradual raising or lowering of the pitch as the song proceeds, unless the singer is able to put himself right later on in the same verse. A very remarkable instance of this may be seen in 'Joan to Jan', which I noted down from a famous old singer in North Devon.

JOAN TO JAN

"I long to be mar-ried," says Joan to Jan. "I have no

boots for to get mar-ried in." "An old pair of boot-legs will do," says

---

[1] It is perhaps of interest to note that when the folk singer refers to singing 'high' he often means 'loud'.

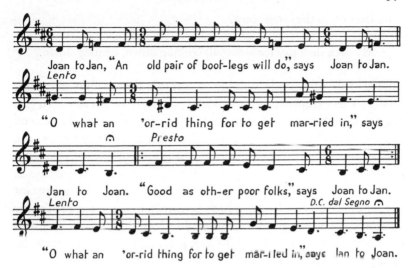

In this song the singer kept his pitch with perfect accuracy, despite the awkward and unvocal interval of the augmented second in the middle of each verse—and he was an old man, too 'in his 74'.

I have already pointed out that the mind of the folk singer is occupied exclusively with the words of what he is singing, with the clearness of which he will allow nothing to interfere. Consequently, he but rarely sings more than one note to a single syllable. Indeed, rather than break this rule, he will often interpolate a syllable of his own, especially when the word in question contains the letter 'l'. For instance the singer of the second version of 'High Germany' (see p. 75) began the first verse as follows:

> O abroad as I was *wordelkin'*
> I was walking all alone
> When I heard a couple *tordelkin'*
> As they walk-ed all along.

Edelin for Ellen, *smodelkin* for smoking, and *cadelico* for calico, are other instances of the same peculiarity.[1] I once noted down the opening line of the well-known song 'Jack Hall' as follows:

> O my name is Jack *Caudle*, chimney sweep, chimney sweep,

[1] The intrusive syllable is particularly prevalent in the singing of gypsies.

and later on in the same song

My neck shall pay for *ordle* (all) coming down, coming down.

This rule of a single syllable to a single note is, however, not without its exceptions. Occasionally, as we have already seen (see p. 31), superfluous notes, for the sake of ornament, are introduced by the singer; and in some songs the third and fourth phrases are linked together by a short passage that is sung to one syllable, as in 'The Ship in Distress' (see p. 92). In the latter case the passage in question is sometimes so extended that it becomes an important vocal flourish or cadenza, which is plainly inserted for expressive reasons. A good example of this may be seen in that very beautiful air 'My Bonnie Boy' (*English County Songs*, p. 146), of which the last phrase runs as follows:

MY BONNIE BOY

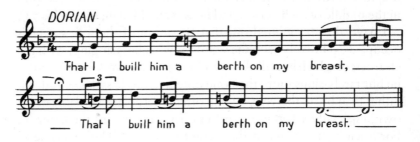

But these are the exceptions that prove the rule, and it may, I think, be taken that the usual habit in folk singing is to sing but one note to each syllable. Perhaps the custom is observed more strictly in some counties than in others.

Most folk singers, beside their own peasant songs, know a certain number of 'composed' songs. Indeed, it is these songs that they will first offer to the collector in the mistaken belief that, like all educated people, he will prefer them to the old-fashioned songs. The popular songs that they thus offer him are not, however, the town songs of today, but of yesterday. At the present time, for instance, the peasants are singing the popular songs of the mid-Victorian era, such as 'Woodman, spare that tree', 'The Mistletoe Bough', 'Cheer boys, Cheer', etc., etc., rather than 'Daisy, Daisy', or 'The Bull and the Bush'. On the other hand, the popular songs of a still earlier period, 1800–1850, if they were ever sung by the peasantry, have long since been forgotten by them. Dibdin's songs, for instance, have almost entirely disappeared. I only know one of them that is still sung in Somerset, and the Rev. S. Baring-Gould tells me that he has only heard two of them in Devon and Cornwall. This is very remarkable when we remember the vogue which they once enjoyed. Dibdin, it will be recalled, was commissioned by the Admiralty to write sea songs for the people, and he complied by turning out 1,300 songs or so in the course of a few years. I have no doubt that many of these were freely sung by the peasant singers of a previous generation, but they have evidently failed to survive the wear and tear of time and usage.

From these considerations we may, I think, reasonably conclude that the popular songs of the town have always been sung to a limited extent by folk singers, side by side with their own songs; although none of the former, apparently, have succeeded in obtaining a permanent resting-place in their affections. And herein the peasant shows his good taste. Give him time, and the folk singer is just as good a critic as your cultivated musician. He sings only what he likes, and though for a while the superficial sweetness of an indifferent tune may beguile him, he will sooner or later inevitably tire of it, and discard it in favour of those tunes whose qualities are more enduring. The town songs have never taken root in the country; they have been ousted in the struggle for existence by the superior and more permanent attributes of the peasant song.

OLD ENGLISH SONGS

Many people confound the folk song proper with what is ordinarily known as the 'Old English' song. The designation 'Old English' is usually employed in a very loose and unscientific manner. It is indifferently applied to three distinct classes of song, *viz.* (1) 'composed' and popular songs of a past epoch, such as 'The Bay of Biscay', 'Rule, Britannia!', or 'The Lass of Richmond Hill'; (2) songs founded upon folk airs and set to words written by professional ballad mongers, such as 'Begone Dull Care', 'The Vicar of Bray', or 'Cease your Funning'; and (3) folk songs that were collected and printed a century or more ago and which were freely edited by contemporary musicians in accordance with the musical notions of their day, such as 'Polly Oliver', or 'Come Lasses and Lads'.

We have just seen that songs belonging to the first of these categories have never enjoyed more than a fleeting popularity with the country singers.

With regard to the songs of the second type, we must bear in mind that the popular town songs of the olden days were nearly always, or at any rate very frequently, set to tunes that were founded upon folk airs. This is no doubt the reason why so many of them have been preserved. The words of 'Lilliburlero' would scarcely have survived two centuries and more, if it had not been for the sterling qualities of the tune to which they were united. The ballad writers of those days showed their wisdom in attaching their words to tunes of proved worth, rather than to the ephemeral compositions of contemporary musicians; we can but regret that such an excellent habit has not survived to the present day. It was not, perhaps, wholly a matter of choice with the ballad writers; for in those days composers were more occupied with the manipulation of themes than with the invention of them. It would be very hard to find a single tune in art music up to the end of the sixteenth century that was wholly the composition of a professed musician; and a very large proportion of the themes embedded in the music of the two following centuries were little more than free adaptations of folk airs. Be this as it may, the old song books are full of what may be called 'derived' folk tunes, many of which have since found their way into the standard collections of Old English airs. That is why, in the absence of collections of genuine folk airs, Old English songs have so often been mistaken for folk tunes.

Of course, the folk tunes under discussion suffered in the process of adaptation. To what extent they were corrupted we can only guess, except in the cases of those tunes which have since been recovered by folk-song collectors. The well-known air 'The Vicar of Bray', for example, was, we must presume, a free rendering, perversion if you will, of 'Country Gardens', a tune which is still in use amongst Morris dancers. The two airs are now printed for purposes of comparison.

THE VICAR OF BRAY

From Chappell's Popular Music

COUNTRY GARDENS

Needless to say, the peasants do not sing and, probably, never have sung 'The Vicar of Bray'. Leaving out of account the tune, which lacks the spontaneity, artlessness and spirit of the genuine folk melody, the words would not appeal to them.

Many of the airs in the ballad operas of the eighteenth century were derived from folk tunes. They were introduced at irregular intervals during the course of the opera, and were set to words in keeping with the situations of the play. *The Beggars' Opera*, the first and most famous of the series, was produced in 1727 and contained sixty-nine songs, most of which were labelled with the titles of folk songs. Gay, the author of the opera, not being himself a musician, engaged the services of a German, Pepusch by name, who noted down and arranged the airs which Gay sang to him. It needs but a cursory examination of this opera to see that the airs are anything but faithful transcriptions of genuine peasant tunes. The ancient dorian air, 'Cold and Raw', is converted into a minor tune with a minor sixth and a sharpened leading note; other modal airs have obviously received similar treatment; while many of the major airs are provided with dominant modulations to bring them 'up to date'. The rhythm of the fine old melody, 'Constant Billy', is changed that it might fit the metre of the new words of 'Cease your Funning', and the tune adorned with a dominant modulation at the middle cadence. A comparison between the edited and the traditional versions of this air will serve to illustrate the nature of the alterations or 'improvements' of which Gay or Pepusch, or both of them, were guilty.

CEASE YOUR FUNNING

From The Beggars' Opera

CONSTANT BILLY

Which of the two authors must be held responsible for the maltreatment of the folk airs contained in *The Beggars' Opera* it is not easy to decide. It is difficult to believe that Pepusch was the culprit. He was a first-rate musician and, unlike his professional brethren, he had a keen affection for, as well as an abstruse knowledge of, the ancient modes upon which subject he was the author of two books. It is inconceivable that such a man would have modernized modal airs, if Gay had sung them to him. On the other hand, it is more than probable that Gay, who was a townsman and therefore stepped in the music of his day, would unconsciously modernize the tunes which he sang to his collaborator. This is not to accuse him of any want of good faith; not being a technical musician, he might easily alter the airs without knowing that he had done so. No collector would accept as authentic a folk air which came to him through the mediation of an educated singer. Be this as it may, it is impossible to accept the tunes in *The Beggars' Opera* as trustworthy records of peasant song; and a like criticism must regretfully be passed upon all the so-called folk airs contained in the forty or more ballad operas which followed upon the heels of *The Beggars' Opera*. Had the musicians who were responsible for the music of the ballad operas but had the grace to present the tunes in their native dress, unadorned and un-'improved', *i.e.* as the peasantry were at that period singing them, the ballad operas of the eighteenth century would now be of incalculable worth, veritable treasure houses of English folk song. As it is, they are but the repositories of tunes which, scientifically speaking, are well-nigh worthless.

Songs that belong to the third category, *i.e.*, edited folk songs, are only to be distinguished from the ballad opera airs, with which we have just dealt, in that their words are of reputed folk origin as well as their tunes. It is hardly necessary to point out that the edited folk song has never penetrated into the country districts. The peasant singers would naturally prefer their own songs as they had themselves fashioned them to the forms in which they came to them from the hands of professional musicians. To the musician of a past age, especially to him of the eighteenth century, the irregular rhythms, the absence of modulations, the unexpected intervals, and the curious modal cadences of the folk tune, were blemishes, gross and shocking; natural enough, he would argue, in the work of un-tutored yokels, but ignorant errors, nevertheless, which must be carefully removed if the tunes were to be made acceptable to the more delicate ears of politer audiences. Needless to say, in the process of editing to which they were thus subjected, the peasant tunes were usually despoiled of just those characteristic qualities from which they derived their unique charm. We cannot, there-fore, without discrimination, accept as genuine folk products the so-called folk tunes which were collected and printed in the eighteenth, seventeenth and earlier centuries. Like the folk airs of the ballad operas, they are suspect; and, if we would stand on firm ground, we must judge English folk song by those examples only which have been taken down from the lips of peasant singers by competent musicians, and published by them without any alterations whatsoever.

Fortunately, it is possible, in some measure, to repair the damage which the narrow pedantry of the past inflicted upon English folk song—in the cases, that is, of those tunes which are still sung in the country districts. Such songs, for instance, as 'Gossip Joan', 'The Shepherd's Daughter', 'The Three Ravens', 'The Baffled Knight', 'Pretty Betsie', 'Admiral Benbow', and many others, are still popular with country singers; but they are all sung in forms other than those in which they appear in collections of 'Old English Airs'. In cases such as these, it is not difficult to distinguish between the genuine folk song and its edited version. There are, no doubt, a few songs which have long been in print, but which, for some reason or other, have happily escaped injury. 'Barbara Ellen' and 'The Maid of Islington', may perhaps be placed in this category, and safely accepted as genuine and unedited folk songs. But these are the exceptions. The majority of those 'Old English' airs which purport to be folk songs compare very unfavourably with the versions of them that are now being collected.

No better nor more typical instance of the difference between the genuine folk air and the 'improved' edition of it could be adduced than 'The Miller of the Dee', already referred to in a preceding chapter. If the reader will carefully examine the form in which this tune is printed in Chappell's *Popular Music of the Olden Time*,

From Chappell's Popular Music

and compare it with the version of the same tune which Dr Vaughan Williams recently noted down from a peasant singer,

Noted by Dr Vaughan Williams

he will see for himself how grievously a fine tune has suffered at the hands of the editing musician.

Curiously enough, Chappell himself, at p. 748 of his *Popular Music*, prints a variant of this tune which he noted down from some street singers in Kilburn, and which, by the way, is one of the very few genuine traditionary airs in his book. The superiority of this second tune over the first does not, however, seem to have struck him; indeed, it may be doubted whether he perceived the connection between the two tunes.

With regard to those songs which are no longer sung by the country singers of today, we must, perforce, be content with the edited versions which have come down to us in the scores of the ballad operas and in old song books. That they are garbled versions cannot decisively be established, of course; although it needs but little discernment to perceive upon most of them the marks of the devastating hand of the editing musician. In 'Come Lasses and Lads', for example, which is one of those songs which are no longer sung by the folk, the modulation to the relative minor at the middle cadence is obviously the addition of a latter-day musician— analogous to the dominant modulations in 'Polly Oliver' and 'Constant Billy', upon which we have already commented.

The above remarks apply, of course, only to those folk airs which have found their way in some form or other into collections of 'Old English Airs'. And these are, comparatively speaking, but few. For we must remember that the vast majority of English folk songs have never been included in these collections in any form whatever, good, bad, or indifferent. Such songs as 'The Banks of the Sweet Dundee', 'The Sweet Primeroses', 'The Dark-Eyed Sailor', 'The Golden Vanity', and scores of others of a similar type, are known and sung by almost every folk singer of the present day. They are the ordinary, typical songs of the English peasant, the ABC of English folk song. And yet not one of these characteristic and beautiful songs was known to musicians until they were recently recovered and published by collectors. How they escaped inclusion in books of English airs which contained so many tunes that were inferior to them must for ever remain a mystery. But, obviously, no publication which excluded them could for one moment be regarded as a representative collection of the folk songs of England.

I have dealt at some length with this question of the exact nature of the 'Old English Song' and its relationship to the genuine peasant ditty, because, until recently, it has been universally accepted as English folk song. In the absence of any published editions of genuine English folk song, taken down directly from the lips of peasant singers, this confusion was excusable. It was a case of 'Old English Songs', or nothing. Although, however, there is happily no longer any excuse for perpetuating it, many musicians still cling to the old superstition. Only the other day, a well-known musician answered the foolish assertion that we had no folk songs in England, by referring to the late Mr William Chappell's *Popular Music of the Olden Time*.

Now Chappell gathered nearly the whole of his material from libraries and museums, and his book contains no more than a stray tune here and there which can properly be classified as folk song. It is emphatically not a collection of folk songs. Its title proclaims that it deals, not with the living songs of today, but with the dead songs of the past. This is not to depreciate the value of the work in question. It contains the results of an immense amount of patient research, presented with a wise discrimination, analysed with scientific acumen, and adorned with rich and deep learning. But it is, avowedly, no more than a record of the printed music of the past. The traditionary ballads of the people, except so far as they appeared in the manuscripts and printed books of past centuries, are practically excluded from it. Chappell himself would not, I think, have quarrelled with this estimate of his work. Indeed, in the second edition, which appeared thirteen or fourteen years ago, the editor, Mr Wooldridge, emphasized the real purpose of the book by carefully excluding the few traditional airs that were contained in the original edition.

As a matter of fact, Chappell had but little sympathy with the folk song collector, of the value of whose recoveries he was profoundly mistrustful. This, no doubt, arose from the fact that he spent the greater part of his life in libraries and museums, and became so accustomed to the handling of manuscripts that he grew suspicious of all evidence but that of the printed or written word. This can be gathered from remarks that he himself makes from time to time in his book, respecting the untrustworthiness of the tunes sung by peasants; as when he points out that the versions of a certain tune collected in different parts of the country 'differ in some points, especially in the terminations of the phrases, *but that might be expected as it was gathered from untutored singers*'.

That this is a just and true estimate of his attitude towards the peasant singers was confirmed the other day by a friend of his, who recorded in the public press that he had once expressed to her the opinion that 'unwritten songs were but corrupt versions of printed copies'. It never seems to have occurred to him that those self-same printed copies, which he handled so reverently and confidently, might, and indeed, probably were, 'corrupt versions' of 'unwritten songs'. The numberless minute variations that are found in the several versions of every traditional peasant song represent to the expert in folk song the causes and conditions of growth, the proofs of vitality, and the surest evidences of authenticity. But to Chappell they simply aroused suspicion.

In conclusion, we must once again warn the student of folk song not to search for his material amongst the printed and manuscript music of the past, nor in the numerous collections of 'Old English

Songs'. He must either go direct to the peasant singers themselves, or to those publications which contain songs that have been taken down from their lips by competent musicians. For his guidance, and for the benefit of all those who are interested in the subject, a list of these books is printed in Appendix I.[1]

[1] This appendix has been amplified and includes collections published after 1907.

CHAPTER X

THE DECLINE OF THE FOLK SONG

FOLK SONGS and folk dances, in days gone by, played an important part in the social life of the English village. That life is now waning, and with it are passing away the old traditions and customs. It is, happily, still possible, here and there, and in out-of-the-way nooks and corners, to come upon peasant men and women old enough to remember the village life of sixty, seventy, or even eighty years ago; and they will sing to you the songs and explain to you the dances that, in their young days, and on summer evenings, were sung and danced on the village greens. The English peasant still exists, although the peasantry as a class is extinct. Reformers would dispel the gloom which has settled upon the countryside, and revive the social life of the villages. Do what they will, however, it will not be the old life that they will restore. That has gone past recall. It will be of a new order, and one that will bear but little resemblance to the old social life of the 'Merrie England' of history.

Already many of the old singers from whom three or four years ago I recovered songs are dead and gone; and, of the rest, few will be able to 'tune a zong' many years hence. Mr Baring-Gould tells me that, without a single exception, all his old singers have gone to their long rest. The seventy-nine songs in *Folk-Songs from Somerset* were contributed by thirty-eight singers, whose ages average over seventy years apiece. In less than a decade, therefore, English folk singing will be extinct.

I have learned that it is, as a rule, only waste of time to call upon singers under the age of sixty. Their songs are nearly all modern; if, by chance, they happen to sing an old one, it is so infected with the modern spirit that it is hardly worth the gathering. There are, of course, exceptions; but they are few. Cripples, and those whose infirmities have kept them within doors engaged in sedentary occupations, sometimes retain the old traditions with greater fidelity than their more fortunate brothers and sisters. But they are not many, and their songs, moreover, are not always trustworthy.

It appears, then, that the last generation of folk singers must have been born not later than sixty or seventy years ago—say 1840. Why the chain of tradition snapped, and without warning, at that particular link, it is difficult to say. Some would attribute it to the invention of railways, to the spread of education, to the industrial revival, or even to the political unrest which followed the passing of the Reform Bill and the repeal of the corn laws. On the other hand, there are those who would ascribe the cause not to an altered environment, but to a fundamental change in the outlook of the people themselves, arising from their attainment of a particular stage of their development. Be this as it may, it is the fact of the decadence of the folk song, not the causes which have led to its decline, with which we are here concerned. And the fact is beyond dispute.

Some critics see in the rejection of the folk song by the country people of the last generation proof that its vitality is exhausted. They argue that the folk song was the product of a society, which, in the natural course of things, has come to an end; that, as the survival of a past age, it has nothing in common with the complexities of modern life. They accordingly ridicule all attempts to popularize the folk song in the towns and the country villages, and would relegate the collectors' gatherings to the museums and libraries for the benefit of antiquarians and archaeologists.

This view, which on the face of it sounds reasonable enough, rests upon the assumption that the country people of the last generation rejected the folk song for the sole reason that it did not attract them nor satisfy their desires so well as the modern music of the towns. This, however, is not really so, as the following incident brought very clearly to my notice a few years ago.

I had collected a large number of songs in Hambridge—from the grandparents, of course—with the co-operation of the Vicar, the Rev. C. L. Marson. We published several of these songs, and the Vicar directed that they should be taught in the village school. The children eagerly received them, and once again the old traditional songs were heard, between school hours, from end to end of the long village street. Then, strangely enough, the fathers and mothers of the schoolchildren pricked up their ears; the old songs caught their fancy. They learned them from their children and sang them with evident pleasure. That is to say, the men and women who forty or fifty years ago had scornfully refused to accept these same songs from their parents were now learning them with avidity from their own children! Clearly, the fault was not with the songs, nor with their attractiveness. This experience does not stand alone. The experiment has since been repeated in other country villages with, in every case, identically the same result.

Again, the decline of the folk song has led some critics to argue that the songs that are now being collected are corrupt and unworthy of serious consideration; that they are, as a well-known musician recently put it, 'the decaying survivals of something better'.

So far as the words are concerned, as we have already seen, this criticism is to some extent justified. A very much better case can, however, be made out for the tunes. The causes, whatever they may have been, which led to the decadence of the words have, happily, operated upon the tunes to a much smaller extent. And this statement is made not forgetting that it is, in the nature of things, less easy to discern corruptions in a tune than in its text. In the latter case the blemishes are patent, and cannot be disguised. But, so long as a tune is clear in its tonality and intelligible in its rhythm, who is to say whether it is true to tradition or not? It may be that many of the tunes now being recovered by collectors are but the veriest travesties of the same tunes as they were sung a hundred years ago; that, in fact, since then, devolution not evolution has been at work. There is, however, not a tittle of evidence to warrant any such supposition; for no one, a hundred years ago, collected our folk tunes, and there is, therefore, nothing with which a comparison can be made. If the tunes have suffered we can but deplore it. In the meanwhile, we must rest satisfied with their face value, and console ourselves with the reflection that, however corrupt they may be, they are, nevertheless, indisputably very fine melodies. For most of us this is enough.[1]

But although, as we have said, it is difficult to test the fidelity of the tradition by which these tunes have been preserved, it is not impossible to offer some evidence bearing upon the point at issue. Here, for instance, is a tune that I collected from a very famous old Mendip singer, Mr James Bishop—now, I regret to say, dead. It is a curious tune and quite unlike any other variant of the same song that I have recovered:

TARRY TROWSERS

First version

Strangely enough Dr Vaughan Williams captured a very close variant of the same air from an Essex singer. This is his version:

Second version

Noted by Dr Vaughan Williams

[1] This paragraph as it stands may give a false impression of what were, in fact, Sharp's views. He is here speaking in general terms of the artistic worth of the folk tunes which had been recovered in his day. He did not fail to recognize that among them there were instances of poor tunes in which devolution had played a part (see pp. 155 and xvii).

It will be seen that the two forms of this air are substantially the same, allowing, of course, for the small differences inherent in tunes that have been evolved and transmitted orally. Now, in the face of such evidence as this, would any critic be bold enough to maintain that either of these versions is a corrupt tune? To do so would involve the assumption that the same tune has been corrupted in substantially the same manner, and to the same extent, in two districts as far apart as the width of southern England. Surely, it is more reasonable to conclude that neither of them is corrupt, but · that both have been handed down to us by a tradition that is beyond suspicion. The reader will recall another and similar instance narrated in a preceding chapter (see p. 22). If further evidence be needed, the Journal of the Folk-Song Society will supply scores of examples of tunes that have been faithfully preserved, in almost identical forms, by singers in different parts of the country.

We have already seen that in the absence of any authentic collection of English folk tunes that were recorded a century or more ago, it is practically impossible to apply the only test which would incontrovertibly settle the question under discussion. I can, however, produce one piece of evidence of this nature. Last year I noted down the following air to 'The Bonny Bunch of Roses, O!' from Mr John Cully at Farrington Gurney, in Somerset:

THE BONNY BUNCH OF ROSES, O!

First version

MIXOLYDIAN

In the current number of the *Folk-Song Journal*, Mr Charles E. D. Waring communicates the following variant, which he noted down from 'an old Nurse at Lyme Regis, about 1852 to 1856':

Second version

Noted by Mr Charles E. Waring

MIXOLYDIAN

The final A and also the E-flat in the sixth bar call for explanation (see *F.S.J.* III, p. 56). In all other respects, however, this tune, which was recorded more than half a century ago, is very nearly identical with that which I noted down in Somerset last summer. Clearly, so far as this particular tune is concerned, no corruption has taken place during the last fifty years.

The two instances above given, without being conclusive, provide, at any rate, some evidence in favour of the trustworthiness of those folk tunes which are now being collected in England.

I have, of course, as all collectors must have done, frequently listened to tunes which were incomplete, that varied verse by verse, and which were obviously corrupt, or imperfectly remembered. But this is not necessarily peculiar to the present generation of singers. The collector of a hundred years ago would probably have found the same thing. Folk singers vary in capacity just as do their professional brethren of the towns. The great ages of the folk singers of today may mean that we hear a larger proportion of corrupt or imperfect tunes than would our predecessors of a century ago—if there had been any. But, after all, it is not difficult to sift the chaff from the grain. The fact that a tune is repeated in every verse makes it possible to judge whether it is a consistent version or not; for, if the singer is hazy about the melody, it is easy enough to convict him in the course of a long ballad.

In seeking for an explanation why the tunes have lasted longer than the words, we must remember that the singer is mentally occupied with the words, but not with the tune, which he sings without conscious effort. Consequently, lack of practice would act more injuriously upon the words than upon the tunes. But another and more important reason arises from the fact upon which we have already commented, that, centuries ago, the words of folk songs were printed on ballad sheets and disseminated all over the country, while the tunes were preserved by oral tradition only. If the words had been carefully collected and accurately printed on the broadsides, this would have aided their preservation. Unfortunately, this was rarely the case.

Usually they were recited, from memory, by the hawkers and pedlars to the ballad printers, by whom they were freely and often unintelligently edited. Moreover, the ballad sheet provided the singers with new sets of words, but not with new tunes. Consequently, the old ballads were often discarded and replaced by more modern sets of words which were, however, sung to old ballad tunes. So that in more ways than one the distribution of ballad broadsides has acted detrimentally upon the words of the old traditional songs, without exerting any injurious effect upon the melodies.

But, as I have already said, the real answer to the critic who is disposed to throw doubts upon the trustworthiness of latter-day folk tunes is to be found in an examination of the tunes themselves. If they are intrinsically beautiful, what matter if they be corrupt or not?

CHAPTER XI

THE ANTIQUITY OF THE FOLK SONG

IT IS an easy matter to assess the age of ordinary composed music. The composer's name is usually upon the title page to bear witness, if not to the exact year of its birth, at least to the period in which it was written. Even where the composition is unsigned, a date can generally be ascribed to it without difficulty.

A study of the history of music will demonstrate that each generation of composers has been occupied with the solution of particular technical and aesthetic problems. Consequently, the music of every epoch is distinguished by the presence of certain musical figures or idioms, which to the musical historian bear evidence of the date at which it was composed. The amateur, for example, will usually ascribe the music of the first half of the eighteenth century to Handel. He recognizes the formal cadences and the four-square type of phrase, with which a passing acquaintance with the *Messiah* or one of the better known oratorios of Handel has familiarized him. He is unaware that these musical idioms were not peculiar to Handel, but were the common characteristics of all the music of the period, by whomsoever composed. Every age has produced its own distinctive type of music.

But when we come to assign a date to folk music, we are faced with a much more difficult problem, perhaps even an insoluble one. For, in one sense, a folk song never grows old. It belongs not to one period but to many; it is always growing. It lives, moreover, upon sufferance. Its life is conditioned by its popularity. If its development is arrested, sooner or later it falls in popular esteem; singers cease to sing it, and it dies beyond hope of resuscitation. It is recorded on no written or printed document, and all the antiquarians in the world are incapable of reviving it. The folk song in this sense, therefore, can never grow old; it must always be abreast of the times. Modernity is the key-note of the folk song. Those who regard the collector as an amiable archaeologist, and ascribe to his recoveries an antiquarian value only, altogether mistake the nature of the folk song.

The folk songs which the country people are now singing may be compared to the acorns which fell last autumn from an oak. The tree is, perhaps, an old one and has its roots in the past, but the acorns are the product of a season's growth. It is just as easy, or just as difficult, to discern the age of the tree by examining its fruit, as it is to assign the birth-year to a folk song by an examination of it in the form in which it is being sung by the present generation of folk singers. Apart from physical signs, the age of a human being can be gauged with tolerable accuracy. With him development and age have proceeded *pari passu*, and the stage of development that he has reached may be compared with that of others whose ages are known. Now the peasant musician has, no doubt, progressed in the practice of his art, generation by generation, but the songs which he now sings represent his present acquirements only. What those same songs were like in their earlier states we do not and never will know, for we have practically no ancient records that are trustworthy. The latter-day folk song does not necessarily bear upon it any mark to witness to its antiquity. One of comparatively recent origin may be indistinguishable from one that has been continuously sung, though in ever varying form, for many centuries. The time expended in the process of composition does not affect the age of the finished product. The theme in the last movement of Beethoven's Choral Symphony cannot be called older than the theme of the first movement, because the former represented the work of a lifetime, while the latter was composed in a few months.

It is often said that a modal folk song must be at least 300 years old, because the modes fell into disuse at the beginning of the seventeenth century. This reasoning is correct enough with respect to art music. It is fallacious when applied to the music of the folk. The common people, as we have seen, were, in all probability, themselves the originators of the modes, and they have never discontinued their use. The mode provides a most efficient instrument for the making of melody, pure and simple; and it is with such melody that the folk are exclusively concerned. It is the peasant idiom, and the folk singer uses it because it fits his purpose, and suits his taste better than any other scale. It is but rarely that a folk singer of the present day will attempt the composition of a folk song. But when he does he will usually and unconsciously fall into one or other of the modes as his natural vehicle of expression. It will also be remembered that the Australian tune is in the mixolydian mode. The mode, in the case of the folk song is, therefore, no test of age.

I have already mentioned that folk singers often show an individual preference for one particular mode. Such singers will unconsciously transpose many of their songs into their favourite scale. The tune of 'Cupid's Garden' is a harmonic melody; it is constructed in a very obvious manner upon the three major chords of the major scale. For this reason it has a very modern flavour. One singer, however, addicted to the dorian mode, sang it to me in his favourite scale. This, to the ear of the art musician, quite disguised its modernity. But it did not make it old. On the other hand, modern characteristics are not necessarily evidence of modern origin, for they may be due to modern influence. The harmonic melody of 'Cupid's Garden' may, therefore, be but an ancient tune in modern garb. I offer no opinion; I give it as an instance of the danger of theorizing about the past history of a folk song.

Again, many people would, *prima facie*, ascribe a great age to a melody apparently as archaic as 'Bruton Town'. It is a song which has, as yet, only been found in Somerset; and I have only heard it sung by three singers, not one of whom can reasonably expect to be alive ten years hence. It may, therefore, be a survival of a past age which has escaped adaptation to the more modern needs of the present race of folk singers and is nearing its end. In this limited sense it may be accounted an old song, *i.e.*, in comparing it with those that have been more continuously subjected to the process of evolution.

It might be conjectured, in cases where the words are of the old ballad type, *e.g.* 'Lady Maisry', 'Earl Richard', etc., that the tunes to which they are sung are of a like age. But it would be unsafe to draw any such deduction. There has been great traffic in tunes, and many an old ballad will be sung to a melody which some singer, not knowing the proper tune, has quite recently fitted to it. The theme of the words of 'The Two Magicians' is, undoubtedly, of ancient origin, but I have grave doubts whether the tune to which I have heard it sung is of any great age.

The fact is, the evidence is too scanty to warrant any certain conclusions with respect to the age of the folk song. We must assume that, of the folk songs now being hardly won from the English peasantry, some have a long history behind them, while others are comparatively of recent birth. And we can only assume as much as this from a general consideration of the manner in which we believe folk songs to have been evolved.

Our inability to ascribe a great age to the folk song will come as a disappointment to those who attach value to a song in proportion to its antiquity. Age and beauty do not necessarily go together with tunes, any more than they do with human beings.

After all, we can but reiterate that the value of the folk song lies in its own intrinsic qualities. If it is beautiful, it needs nothing to recommend it. And if it is not beautiful, declaring it to be as old as Moses will not make it so.

CHAPTER XII

THE FUTURE OF
THE ENGLISH FOLK SONG

THE OPINION has been freely expressed that the recent recoveries of English folk song are destined to create a revolution in the musical taste of this country. This, time alone can show. But it is certain that the sudden and unexpected discovery of an immense mass of melody, not only rich in emotion, but possessing withal a distinctive and national flavour, cannot fail to produce some effect upon the musical life of England.

The Englishman's habit of self-depreciation has often occasioned remark. It is one of those national traits that is exceedingly difficult to account for. For centuries we have rested under the stigma of being an unmusical race, and, so far from resenting the imputation, we have modestly acquiesced. So long as it was believed that we alone of all the nations of Europe possessed no folk music of our own, it was, perhaps, a little difficult to do aught else. It was not enough to point to our 'Old English Songs' in refutation of the charge, because, beautiful as many of them are, they are obviously lacking in those especial qualities which characterize the folk songs of other countries. Now, however, that recent research has shown that in this respect we are at least as richly endowed as any other European nation, the case is materially altered.

But it is early days, and English folk song has yet to win its spurs. For even now, when at last the folk song collector has laid bare the facts and exposed the hollowness of the ancient superstition, the old prejudice still persists. A few enthusiasts, it is true, have become converts, but the majority, including many in high places, have turned deaf ears to the new gospel and still slumber on in the old misbelief.

It is the old story. The habit of self-depreciation, and the in-grained belief that nothing of musical value can come out of

England, have distorted our judgement and blinded our eyes. If we look back, for a moment, upon the past history of music in England, it will, perhaps, help us to understand why we have come to adopt this pessimistic attitude towards the musical prospects of our country.

First of all, we must remember that for centuries past it has been the fashion in England to honour the foreign and decry the native-born musician. Under such conditions no art could flourish. It is not surprising, therefore, that we have had no musician of the first rank since the death of Purcell in 1695. And even Purcell was not uninfluenced by the prevailing beliefs of his day, for he found it necessary to look abroad and—to use his own words—'to endeavour a just imitation of the most famed Italian masters'.

Prior to Purcell, however, musical England held a proud position among the nations of Europe. Her madrigal composers of the sixteenth and early seventeenth centuries were unsurpassed, while her writers of sacred music of the same period stood very nearly as high in the estimation of Europe. Erasmus, writing in 1509, said of the English that 'they challenge the prerogative of having the most handsome women, of keeping the best tables, and of being the most accomplished in the skill of music of any people'. In still earlier days, we were known as 'Merrie England', and renowned throughout Europe as a nation of dancers and ballad singers; and during the infancy of art music we contributed our full share to its nourishment.

But with the death of Purcell English music fell upon evil days. To disparage that which was of native growth, and to applaud all that was French or Italian, became the prevailing fashion. The patronage of the great was bestowed exclusively upon foreign singers and foreign instrumentalists, while English composers and performers were quietly ignored—and those were the days when art was far more dependent upon patronage than, happily, it is now.

Dr Burney (1726–1814), in his history of music, accurately reflected the jaundiced estimate of English music that was customary in his day. Throughout his history he systematically depreciated English music in order that he might the more easily glorify the Italian. In one well-known passage he remarked that 'the Turks have a limited number of tunes, to which the poets of their country have continued to write for ages; and the vocal music of our own countrymen seems long to have been equally circumscribed, for, till the last century, it seems as if the number of our secular and popular melodies did not exceed that of the Turks', which, in a footnote, he stated were exactly twenty-four in number.

The nineteenth century, so rich in the domain of literature, poetry and the sciences, brought to light no English musician of real eminence. During the first half of the century there was no composer of higher rank than Bishop, while, later on, Benedict and Costa, both of foreign extraction, ruled the musical world. Sterndale Bennett, it is true, was a composer of far greater eminence than any of these, and he might, perhaps, have founded an English School of composition had conditions been more favourable. But, although his music was by no means lacking in individuality, it was clearly dominated by the writings of his German contemporaries, and there was little in it that could justly be regarded as distinctive of the country of his birth.

At the present day, there are several English musicians who, in musical ability, scholarship, and technical accomplishment, far outshine any of their predecessors of the previous century. But their warmest admirers must admit that they have as yet written nothing that can be called distinctively English music.[1] And this is, perhaps, natural enough, when it is remembered that, in the absence of an English tradition, they have been compelled to seek their inspiration from abroad, and to mould their styles upon those of their foreign contemporaries.

The fact is, of course, that there exists at the present day no National School of English music. Since the death of Purcell, as we have seen, the educated classes have patronized the music of the foreigner, to the exclusion of that of the Englishman. Foreign vocalists, singing in a foreign tongue, have for two centuries monopolized the operatic stage; while English concert platforms have, during the same period, been exclusively occupied by alien

[1] See Ralph Vaughan Williams's *Appreciation*, p. vii.

singers and instrumentalists, singing and playing the compositions of European writers.

This is the fact. Is this deplorable state of things to continue indefinitely? Is there no remedy? Is England, the land of Shakespeare, to go down to posterity as the only nation in all Europe incapable of original musical expression? Or, is there any justification for the more comforting prediction that the recent recoveries of English folk song—of music, that is, which is disdistinctively national and English, and, therefore, inherently different from that of every other nation in the world—will eventually lead to the foundation of an English National School of composition, comparable with any one of the great Continental schools of music? Let us consider the point.

Some critics, it should be noted, dispute the need of a National School of music in England, and deny that any good results would follow upon its establishment. They argue that music is an universal language, and that national characteristics are elements of weakness rather than of strength, in that they tend to destroy its catholicity and restrict its appeal.

This objection, however, expresses no more than a half-truth. Manifestly, all music written in the conventional forms adopted by the nations of Western Europe may be called universal in the sense that it is intelligible to all musicians irrespective of nationality. At the same time, the products of every existing school of music are characterized by certain attributes which are essentially and demonstrably national. Indeed, it would be difficult to cite a single instance of a school of art or of literature of which this could not be said.

There is no mistaking German music for French, or French for Italian music; although the music of each may make an appeal that reaches beyond the limits of its own country. The truth is, that although in one sense the musician speaks in a universal language, he, nevertheless, betrays his nationality in his music every whit as much as he does in his speech. Music is a medium of expression analogous to that of language, and, although its range may be less restricted than that of speech, it is itself bound by certain national limitations. Hence it follows that no school of music has yet arisen and flourished in Europe that has not primarily been concerned with the expression of national aspirations. Music may be so individual that it will appeal only to the few. If it is to become popular its circle must be widened; and if it is to found or advance a school, it must express the ideals and aspirations that are shared by those to whom it is especially addressed, and be couched in an idiom that is intelligible to them. That is to say, it must possess national attributes, and be to some extent a communal, as opposed to an individual, utterance.

Now we have seen that the earliest form of music, folk song, is essentially a communal as well as a racial product. The natural musical idiom of a nation will, therefore, be found in its purest and most unadulterated form in its folk music. There is no music, for example, so characteristic of the German people as German folk song; of the Russian people as Russian folk music, and so on. The relation, therefore, between German or Russian art music and German or Russian folk music must be a close and intimate one. That much we may assume *a priori*, without seeking further afield for confirmation.

That the German school of art music has been built upon a foundation of German folk song is obvious enough, and is admitted on all hands. The Schubert song, the Weber opera, and the Beethoven symphony have one and all sprung from German folk song. Indeed, this has been freely conceded by German musical writers and critics—Wagner, for example, in his prose writings, has pointed it out over and over again. Some composers, such as those above mentioned, have derived their inspiration directly from folk song; while others, by building upon the music of their predecessors, have only touched upon it indirectly. But that German music, as a whole, has its roots in German folk song, and that it derives its distinctive and national qualities therefrom, there can be no question.

This is also true of the music of the Italian School. No more than a cursory examination of Italian folk song is needed to perceive the relationship that it bears to the dominant-tonic

melodies of Bellini, Donizetti, Verdi, and their followers.[1]
The comparatively recent birth of a national school of music in
Russia provides another example. Its founder was Glinka (1803—
1857), who was called by Liszt the 'prophet-patriarch' of Russian
music. He grew up steeped in the folk music of his own country,
and, early in life, conceived the idea of composing a national opera.
This ambition he eventually satisfied in *The Life of the Tsar* (1836),
an opera which marked an epoch in the musical history of Russia.
As Mrs Newmarch has said:

> The more thoughtful critics saw that the opera was new in the best
> sense of the word, and marked a fresh departure in Art—the birth of a
> genuine School of Russian music. . . . He did not merely play with
> local colour, but re-cast the primitive speech of the folk-song into a
> new and polished idiom, so that henceforth Russian music was able
> to take its place among the distinctive schools of Western Europe.
> (Grove's *Dictionary*.)[2]

Russian composers subsequent to Glinka have worthily carried
on the national tradition founded by him, and the Russian school of
music is now fully the equal of that of any European nation. It is
worthy of remark that Tchaikovsky, perhaps the greatest of the
composers of the new Russian school, did not derive his inspiration
directly from the folk songs of his own country. Madame Lineff,
the eminent Russian folk song collector, has told us that Tchaikovsky is 'full of popular melodies, although, according to his own
confession, he was little acquainted with folk songs.' This is highly
significant. For it shows that when some musician of genius has
once demonstrated how the people's music may be translated into
terms of art music, the musical idiom of the nation is settled once
for all, and may be utilized and developed by composers of the
same nationality, even when, as in the case of Tchaikovsky, they
are themselves ignorant of their country's folk music.
The birth of the Russian school of music is extraordinarily

---

[1] The fine collections of Italian folk song which have recently been made in the remote
countryside show that it covers a much wider range of modality than the folk song that
would have been known to these composers.
[2] 1927 ed. II, p. 395.

interesting to us. It was founded, within living memory, by one man—it may almost be said to have sprung from one opera—and its growth has been so swift, and so recent, that it is possible to examine with the greatest minuteness every stage in its history. For us in England it has many lessons.

Another, and still more modern instance, is furnished by the rise of the Scandinavian school of music. Gade, the first Norwegian composer to win a European reputation, after studying music in his own native land, spent several years at Leipzig. There he became the disciple, first of Schumann, and afterwards of Mendelssohn, and thenceforth wrote music that was German rather than Norwegian. In this way, he disappointed the hopes that his talents had aroused, and he failed to contribute anything of moment towards the foundation of a school of music in his own country. This honour was reserved for Grieg. Unlike Gade, Grieg studied in Leipzig and then returned to Norway, where he became associated with those who were 'devoting themselves to a distinctively national form of the various arts'. Under this influence, he set to work to lay the foundations of a national school of music. He drank deeply at the fount of folk song, with the result that his music 'owes much of its success to the skill with which he adapted the classical structure to themes so nearly allied to actual traditional tunes as to be hardly distinguishable from genuine folk music.' (Groves' *Dictionary*)'[1]

To return to English music. We have seen that, from the age of Purcell down to recent days, music in England has been in the hands of the foreigner. How this came about need not concern us here. It may or may not have proceeded—as the Reverend S. Baring Gould has suggested—from the 'affectation that dated from the period when it was considered proper for a gentleman to make the grand tour. He returned from the Continent to turn up his nose at his old English manor house, and to call in Italian architects to tear it down and substitute for it a Florentine palazzo.'

Some writers attribute the decadence of English music to puritan rather than to foreign influence. They, however, who

[1] 1927 ed. II, p. 459.

espouse this view, should remember that both Germany and Norway were subjected in some degree to a like influence without, in either case, its hindering the foundation of a national school of music. Furthermore, the puritans in England, although they tried their best to do so, never silenced the ballad singer; nor did they succeed in arresting the development of the kindred arts of literature, poetry and painting. Bearing these facts in mind, while we cannot wholly ignore the injurious effect which the puritans, for a while, undoubtedly exerted upon English music, it seems unjust to attribute its decadence wholly to their malign influence.[1]

But, whatever the reason, we cannot blink the fact that, about the time of Charles I, music in England began to languish and to fall from its high estate, until, by the beginning of the nineteenth century, it had become practically moribund.

The question of vital importance for us now to consider is whether English music is capable of resuscitation. One thing is certain; the present vogue of training English musicians to lisp in the tongue of the foreigner can have no beneficial outcome. It is, emphatically, not that way that salvation lies. Nor, on the other hand, need we listen to the pessimists. They, like the poor, are always with us, and will never weary of reminding us that we are an unmusical race, that we have no temperament, and so forth. We may safely turn a deaf ear to such croakings and console ourselves with two considerations.

First of all, we must never forget that, in the past, we proved ourselves capable of holding our own side by side with the foremost of the musical nations of Europe. Unless, therefore, we have since deteriorated, we may reasonably believe in our capacity to repeat in the future what we have accomplished in the past. And, secondly, we must remember that we have a literature of folk song of our own, which affords incontrovertible evidence that, as a nation, we possess a natural and inherent musical faculty of no mean order. The tree, therefore, is sound at the root. If in past

---

[1] In *The Puritans and Music* (Oxford University Press, 1934), Percy Scholes brings evidence to show that the alleged damage to music by the Puritans has been greatly exaggerated.

seasons it has failed to flourish, to put forth branches and leaves and to bear fruit, this is not from any lack of vitality, but simply because it has been neglected, because it has not received the necessary attention and cultivation, because, in short, of the faults of its environment.

So long as we believed that we were barren of folk song, it must be confessed that the musical prospects of the nation looked black. It seemed extremely difficult to credit ourselves with any musical ability comparable with that of other European nations, if, unlike theirs, our peasantry were unable to express themselves in terms of dance and song. Seeing, too, that every school of music on the Continent had been founded upon folk song, how were we English to follow their example if we had not the material with which to build? How were we to make bricks without straw?

Now, however, that this disability has been removed, there is surely no reason for despondency. On the contrary, is there not every reason to regard the future with great hopefulness? We have the musical ability, and we have the folk song. Our first and obvious duty is to see that the latter is restored to the nation as soon as may be; for not until this has been done can we look for results. When every English child is, as a matter of course, made acquainted with the folk songs of his own country, then, from whatever class the musician of the future may spring, he will speak in the national musical idiom.

It is not enough to 'play with local colour'. Brahms did not write Hungarian music when he borrowed Hungarian themes. Nor did Beethoven write Russian quartets when he made use of Russian folk song. Both Brahms and Beethoven wrote German music always, because they were Germans and had been brought up in the traditions of German music. Similarly, the English musician will not necessarily write English music simply by going to English folk music for his themes. It is highly desirable that he should do so; what effect it has upon him will be all in the right direction, and it will, at least, aid in popularizing English folk song. But an English school of music is not going to be founded in that way. For that we must wait until the younger generations have been familiarized with folk song. We must leave it to them to restore English music to its rightful position—to do for our country what Glinka and his followers did for theirs. That we have lain fallow, musically speaking, for two or more centuries is all in our favour. There is nothing so fertile as virgin soil.

Looking forward to the dawn of a new musical era in England brings to mind the precedent of Percy's *Reliques*. It would be difficult to exaggerate the effect upon English poetry which the publication in 1765 by Bishop Percy of five and forty folk ballads occasioned. It not only killed at one blow the cold formalism which had characterized the poetry of the preceding age, but it led to the revival of a taste for genuine and natural poetry which has endured to the present day. Contemporary writers testified to the strength of the new force. Sir Walter Scott recorded:

> The first time I could scrape a few shillings together—which were not common occurrences with me—I bought unto myself a copy of the beloved volumes, nor do I believe I ever read a book half so frequently or with half the enthusiasm.

And Wordsworth's testimony was no less unequivocal:

> I do not think that there is one able writer in verse at the present day, who would not be proud to acknowledge his obligations to the 'Reliques'. I know it is so with my friends [amongst whom, of course, Coleridge and Southey must be included] and for myself, I am happy to make a public avowal of my own.

It is surely not unreasonable to anticipate a similar revival in English music, consequent upon the influence exerted upon musicians of the present generation by the folk songs which are now being collected and published.

But there are other uses, leading to other and no less important results, to which the folk song may be put. There is, for instance, its value as an educational force.

The importance of music as a factor in general education has latterly received almost universal recognition. Educationalists are agreed that the inclusion of music in the curriculum of the elementary school will not only tend to cultivate a taste for music, but will also, by exciting and training the imagination, react beneficially upon character. That some art should, if possible, be taught in the elementary school is highly desirable, if for no other reason than that it may correct the materializing tendencies of those subjects which appeal to the intellect only.

Now it happens that music is the only art that a child can practise without previous study or the acquisition of any technical accomplishment. He can sing and enter into the full aesthetic enjoyment of music without knowing a crotchet from a quaver. Moreover, children are extraordinarily susceptible to music, and display, even in the nursery, an eager desire to sing. It is these considerations which make music a valuable and, in some respects, a unique educational instrument.

Tune is the natural foundation of musical education. The world made tunes for centuries before it made harmony, and the wise educationalist, bearing this in mind, will prescribe melody, and melody only, for the musical education of very young children. With this conclusion few will be found to differ. When we come, however, to the consideration of the songs that shall be used in the school, we tread controversial ground.

The ideal school song should satisfy two conditions. It should, of course, be music of the highest and purest quality. But this is not enough. It must also be attractive to children and be easily assimilated by them. Many, perhaps most, of the songs that are now sung in our elementary schools satisfy one or other of these requirements; few satisfy both. Good music is often dull to children, difficult to sing, and difficult to understand; while the music which is immediately attractive to them is often little better than rubbish. These considerations point to the folk song as the ideal musical food for very young children. Folk songs most certainly belong to the category of good music; they are natural, pure and simple. They are, moreover, attractive to children, easily comprehended, and easily learned by them. The songs must, of course, be chosen

G

with discrimination; the compass of the tunes must be within the range of young voices, and the words adapted to the understanding of immature minds. Above all, they must be of the same nationality as that of the children: English folk songs for English children, not German, French, or even Scottish or Irish.

Historically, as we have seen, folk music came first and provided the foundations upon which the superstructure of art music was subsequently reared. For this reason alone, folk music is clearly the best and the most natural basis upon which to found a musical education. If the songs are carefully graded, beginning with traditional nursery rhymes and advancing by slow degrees to the more difficult folk songs, no other musical pabulum will be needed until the child has reached the age of ten or eleven years. By that time folk music will have served its purpose, and the child will be prepared to make a wider excursion into the realms of art music.

Other nations have, long ago, recognized the value of the folk song in elementary education. Hitherto, from lack of the necessary material, we have been debarred from following the example set by our continental neighbours. Now, however, that we possess that material in abundance, we have no longer any excuse for refusing to follow in their footsteps.[1]

If some such scheme as this which we have been considering were adopted in the State schools throughout the country, and in the preparatory schools of the upper and middle classes as well, not only would the musical taste of the nation be materially raised, but a beneficent and enduring effect would be produced upon the national character. For good music purifies, just as bad music vulgarizes; indeed, the effect of music upon the minds of children is so subtle and so far-reaching that it is impossible to exaggerate the harmful influence upon character which the singing of coarse and vulgar tunes may have. Up till now, the street song has had an open field; the music taught in the schools has been hopelessly beaten in the fight for supremacy. But the mind that has been fed upon the

---

[1] In 1960, Zoltán Kodály writes: 'It is for educated people to adopt and protect traditions, making them an active part in their lives. How this may be done may best be seen in England and Russia.' (*Folk Music of Hungary*, London 1960.)

pure melody of the folk will instinctively detect the poverty-stricken tunes of the music-hall, and refuse to be captivated and deluded by their superficial attractiveness. Good taste is, perhaps, largely a matter of environment; but it is also the result of careful and early training. Matthew Arnold somewhere recommends retaining in the memory certain passages of poetry of undoubted and admitted excellence, to be used as touchstones with which to preserve a high standard of poetical taste. The same will be done with regard to music, if schoolteachers will but adopt a wise and intelligent scheme of musical education, and give their children nothing but the best music, and music, moreover, that they like and can understand; and these conditions can best be satisfied by giving them the folk songs of their own country.

We may look, therefore, to the introduction of folk songs in the elementary schools to effect an improvement in the musical taste of the people, and to refine and strengthen the national character. Our system of education is, at present, too cosmopolitan; it is calculated to produce citizens of the world rather than Englishmen. And it is Englishmen, English citizens, that we want. How can this be remedied? By taking care, I would suggest, that every child born of English parents is, in its earliest years, placed in possession of all those things which are the distinctive products of its race. The first and most important of these is the mother tongue. Its words, its grammatical constructions, its idioms, are all characteristic of the race which has evolved them, and whose ideas and thoughts they are thus peculiarly fitted to express. The English tongue differs from the French or German precisely as the Englishman differs from the Frenchman or the German. Irish patriots are fully alive to this, and, from their own point of view, are quite right in advocating the revival of the Irish language.

Then there are the folk tales, legends, and proverbs, which are peculiar to the English; the national sports, pastimes, and dances also. All these things belong of right to the children of our race, and it is as unwise as it is unjust to rob them of this their national inheritance.

Finally, there are the folk songs, those simple ditties which have sprung like wild flowers from the very hearts of our countrymen, and which are as redolent of the English race as its language. If every English child be placed in possession of all these products, he will know and understand his country and his countrymen far better than he does at present; and knowing and understanding them he will love them the more, realize that he is united to them by the subtle bond of blood and of kinship, and become, in the highest sense of the word, a better citizen, and a truer patriot.

There is still another and wide field to exploit. We are too apt to forget the needs of those tens of thousands of our countrymen who regard music simply from the point of view of melody, who never get beyond something which they can sing, a tune that they can whistle or tap their umbrellas to. All of these are, of course, in the elementary stage of musical education. The pity of it is that the majority of them remain there all their lives, lingering with their feet on the lowest rung of the ladder. It is only the few, the very few, who rise from the bottom and win their way to higher things. And the reason, of course, is that the tunes that attract them, and which they habitually sing, are bad tunes and, therefore, un-educative.

The important thing to remember, and one that would-be reformers too often forget, is that bad tunes are popular, not because of their badness, but because of their attractiveness. The classes who sing bad tunes sing them simply because they never hear good ones that appeal to them with equal force. They are never called upon to exercise a choice. It is a case of bad tunes or nothing. Place, however, good tunes into competition with bad ones, and the good tunes will win the day, provided that—and this is the essential condition—they are at least as 'catchy' and attractive as the bad ones.

Now one of the most remarkable qualities of the folk song is its power of appeal to the uncritical, to those who, unversed in the subtleties of musical science, yet 'know what they like'. Its value lies in its possession of this dual quality of excellence and attractive-ness. Flood the streets, therefore, with folk tunes, and those who now vulgarize themselves and others by singing coarse music hall songs will soon drop them in favour of the equally attractive but far better tunes of the folk. This will make the streets a pleasanter place for those who have sensitive ears, and will do incalculable good in civilizing the masses. Not only will the streets of towns and cities be purged, but those of country villages also. A few weeks ago I was hunting for songs on Exmoor, and had spent two or three hours one afternoon listening to and noting down several exquisite melodies that were sung to me by an old man, eighty-six years of age. In the evening of the same day, my peace was rudely disturbed by the raucous notes of coarse music-hall songs, shouted out, at the tops of their voices, by the young men of the village, who were spending the evening in the bar of my hotel. The contrast between the old-fashioned songs and kindly manners of my friend the old parish clerk who lived hard by and the songs and uncouth behaviour of the present occupants of the bar struck me very forcibly, and threw into strong relief the deplorable deterioration that, in the last thirty years or so, has taken place in the manners and amusements of the country villagers.

It is, however, not only to the uncritical that the folk song makes its especial appeal. There are those who have always been attracted by music and who, being cultivated people, perhaps versed in one of the sister arts, have had the good sense to perform and listen to nothing but the best music; but who, nevertheless, have never been really moved by it. This may be because they began their musical education at the wrong end, with advanced and complex harmonized compositions, instead of with simple melody. To such people, the advent of the folk song has been a revelation. Its pure and simple strains, appealing less to the intellect than to the emotions, have struck home, gone straight to their hearts, and caused many of them to realize for the first time what music really means. To cultivated people such as these the folk song will be an education, helping them to appreciate the beauties of the more advanced modern music which hitherto they have only dimly apprehended.

The views elaborated above will not, of course, be accepted without question.

They are, however, something more than mere theories. Many of them have been wholly and logically deduced from actual experience; others have, in part, been tested and verified by experiment.

Folk songs have already been introduced into many elementary schools, and have, so far without exception, achieved results which confirm our predictions in the most emphatic manner. School-teachers have one and all testified to this. The children, they have said, learn the songs, both words and music, with an ease that astonishes, and this, too, in spite of the fact that many of the songs are modal, irregular in rhythm and, technically speaking, far more difficult than the average school song. What is still more important —and here the evidence is overwhelming—the children sing the songs out of lesson time, in the playground and in the streets; consequently, songs taught in one class soon spread throughout the school, and beyond the school. The children, so at least their teachers say, accept the songs with enthusiasm and regard them as a possession, seeming instinctively to realize that they belong to them of right.

That folk songs, moreover, appeal just as strongly to the more educated classes, has been abundantly proved. For results similar to those recounted above have followed their introduction into pre-paratory schools, public schools, and the universities. That they are popular, too, with the general public is shown by the fact that many of our leading vocalists are now singing them at concerts and vocal recitals.

The evidence, so far as it goes, is decisive; although, of course, it cannot and does not cover the whole ground. It establishes, how-ever, the fact that folk songs are easily learned and readily as-similated by children and adults of all classes; that they exercise over them a peculiar fascination, and appeal to them in a manner which is very wonderful and very different from that produced by any other kind of music. Whether the popularity which folk songs so quickly win will persist, and whether the effects upon taste and character will prove to be as beneficial as we have predicted, are questions which time alone can answer. But it is surely not unreasonable to credit with the quality of endurance songs that have stood the test of centuries of wear and tear; nor hazardous to assume that good tunes will, of a surety, exercise a salutary influence upon the minds and characters of those who sing them.

Every week adds to the accumulation of the evidence in support of our contention that the re-introduction of folk songs into England will effect many and notable reforms.

It becomes, therefore, a matter of the highest interest to enquire what steps are being taken to bring about this desirable consummation. Up to the present, all that has been done has been effected by private and individual effort. Upon a population so large as that of England, a small band of reformers, however enthusiastic, cannot make a great impression, at any rate in a moment. And the matter is urgent: time can ill be spared. If anything really effective is to be done, it must be done at once, and on an adequate scale. Seeing that the elementary schools are the key of the position, the Board of Education would seem to be the proper authority to undertake the work. If a decree were to issue from Whitehall, recommending—for there is no power to compel— that English folk songs be freely taught in the primary schools throughout the country, the problem would be more than half solved.[1]

But if the Board of Education take any action in the matter, it must, to be effective, be based upon the theory propounded in the foregoing pages. That is to say, the authorities must realize that the folk song stands in a category of its own, that it is generically distinct from all other forms of music, and that, as such, it must be given a special place in the educational scheme. Any action which they may take, and which fails to recognize this, is, I am convinced, foredoomed to failure.

The spectacle of a great nation, like England, in an advanced stage of civilization, intent upon the instruction of her people in their own folk songs, is a strange one. Here is a country with its folk

---

[1] In later years, the Board (now Ministry) of Education whole-heartedly supported the teaching of English folk songs in schools. In 1919, the Board appointed Sharp as Occasional Inspector of Training Colleges in Folk-Song and Dancing.

music neglected or ignored for a century and more; its folk singers, for the greater part, dead or mute; its musicians, many of them, found declaring that English folk music is negligible or non-existent; its children growing up, generation after generation, having never heard the songs that to their forefathers were the songs of life itself. In all this, we have in England today a spectacle, likely enough, unique in the history of the world.

Small wonder the English are called, even by the cultivated and shrewd amongst themselves, greatly lacking or altogether unoriginal in the musical sense. As I have already shown, in every country—certainly in every European country—where the music is native and sincere, expressive of the soul and aspirations of its people, there also the children have grown to maturity with the folk music of their own country a sound as familiar to their ear as the sound of their mother tongue itself. To ourselves as a nation, the sound of our folk music is all but unknown. And, in place of it, we have been nurtured musically—rather, unmusically—upon alien sounds, or sounds fugitive and flashy, or pretty and insincere, or ugly and downright harmful.

The task that lies before the reformer is a formidable one. Apathy, ignorance, and prejudice, encumber the path. There is, moreover, one especial difficulty, which he would do well to realize. The practice of folk singing in England has, for very many years, been confined exclusively to one small class of the community. The folk song will, therefore, come to the majority of the nation unhallowed by past associations, with nothing to recommend it but its own intrinsic qualities.

Now this is a very serious disability. For one of the reasons why the German, for instance, is so attached to his *Volkslieder*, is that he has known them all his life. They are intimately associated with every stage in his career. They were the first songs that he heard in the nursery, and they were the first songs that he learned to sing. It was through the doors of the folk songs of his country that he entered the great world of music. The history of his country, too, is in some measure bound up with his folk songs. They have been sung on great historical occasions, at times of his country's triumph, or, maybe, at moments of national grief, and the associations which have in this way grown up around them, account, in no small degree, for the feelings of patriotism which they inspire, and the affection in which they are held by him. A wealth of association clings around them. Over and above their aesthetic qualities, and independently of any national appeal they may make, they represent to him something which we, who are learning our folk songs in middle life, can never know.

If the efforts that are now being made to popularize it are successful, similar associations will, no doubt, and in the course of time, cluster around the English folk song also. In the meanwhile it comes to us destitute of association, unlinked with the past; like an ancient building newly restored, with walls scraped and cleaned and stripped of their moss and fern.

Nevertheless, this is a defect which time will cure. In the meanwhile, the English folk song, if it is to win the affections of the nation, must do so upon its own merits. Being the product of a past era, it possesses a historical and archaeological value which will commend it to some. It has also, as we have seen, certain national characteristics which must render it especially acceptable to English ears. But it is not merely on these, or upon any sentimental grounds, that the resuscitation of the English folk song is here advocated. The question is, rather: Is it worth reviving? In other words, is it, apart from all other considerations, beautiful in itself, judged as music, pure and simple, and judged, too, by the very highest standard?

Now, this is a question of taste rather than of argument. For this reason, we have, in the foregoing pages, dwelt but little upon the aesthetic qualities of our folk music. And yet no recommendation could be stronger than one that is founded upon artistic considerations. There are not so many fair things in the world that no room can be found for more. In a material age, too, such as the present, there is an especial need for fostering the growth and development of those things which, like good music, exercise a purifying and regenerative influence. If, therefore, the English folk song is, as I fervently believe it to be, music of the very highest quality, that alone is sufficient justification for advocating its revival. And where is the musician who could listen unmoved to such exquisite melodies as 'The Seeds of Love', 'My Bonny Boy', 'Bushes and Briars', 'Henry Martin', or 'The Trees they do grow high'[1]—to mention the first that come to mind? Surely, such tunes as these may safely challenge comparison with the greatest melodies that any European country has produced.

If this be sound criticism, it is only necessary that the folk song of our country should be known for it to win for itself an abiding resting place in the hearts of the people. As time goes on, it will, no doubt, become enriched by the associations which will gradually gather around it. And then, but not before, will the English people enter once again into the full possession of their musical heritage.

---

[1] The texts of these songs and three others are given in Appendix II together with the tunes that have not been quoted in the body of the work.

BIBLIOGRAPHY

COLLECTIONS OF ENGLISH FOLK SONG WHICH HAVE BEEN TAKEN DOWN DIRECTLY FROM THE LIPS OF FOLK SINGERS[1]

NOTE The following abbreviations have been used in the foregoing pages:—
F.S.F.S. — *Folk Songs from Somerset*
F.S.J. — *Journal of the Folk-Song Society*
Selected Edition — *English Folk Songs Selected Edition*

NOTED BY CECIL SHARP

1904–19 *Folk Songs from Somerset*, 5 parts. (Parts 1–3 with C. L. Marson.) The Wessex Press, Taunton. 130 songs. (Out of print. Most of the songs are included in *English Folk Songs, Selected Edition*, or *Folk Songs for Schools*, published by Novello.)

1905–27 *Journal of the Folk-Song Society*. Vol. II, No. 6, 1905. Vol. V, No. 18, 1914. Vol. V, No. 20, 1916. Vol. VIII, No. 31, 1927. 214 songs without accompaniment. (Can be obtained from the English Folk Dance and Song Society, Cecil Sharp House, Regents Park Road, London N.W.1.)

1906 *English Folk Songs for Schools* (with S. Baring-Gould). Curwen, London. 52 songs.

1908–22 *Folk Songs for Schools*, 9 parts. Novello, London. 118 songs, most of which appear in *Folk Songs from Somerset*, or other publications.

1911 *English Folk Carols*. Novello, London. 21 songs.

1912 *Folk Songs from Various Counties*. Novello, London. 12 songs.

1914 *English Folk Chanteys*. Schott, London. 60 songs.

1921–3 *English Folk Songs, Selected Edition*, 2 parts. Novello, London. 100 songs, of which all but 10 appear in earlier publications. Reprinted in one volume 1959.

Folk Songs of English Origin Collected in America

1932 *English Folk Songs from the Southern Appalachian Mountains*, edited by Maud Karpeles. Oxford University Press, London. 2 vols. 1932. 971 songs. Reprinted 1960 in one volume. Part of this

---

[1] See also *A Guide to English Folk Song Collections* by Margaret Dean-Smith. University of Liverpool Press, 1954.

collection was originally published with Olive Dame Campbell by G. P. Putnam, New York, 1917.
Selected from above:
Folk Songs of English Origin, 2 parts. Novello, London. 1919, 1921. 26 songs.
and
Nursery Songs from the Appalachian Mountains, 2 parts. Novello, London. 1921, 1923. 55 songs.

NOTED BY OTHER COLLECTORS

1843   *Sussex Songs*, collected and printed for private circulation by John Broadwood. 16 songs. Reprinted with additions collected by Lucy Broadwood. The whole arranged by H. F. Birch Reynardson. Stanley, Lucas, Weber, London. 1889. 26 songs.

1877   *Nursery Rhymes and Country Songs*, M. H. Mason. Metzler, London. 57 songs.

1882   *Northumbrian Minstrelsy*, J. C. Collingwood Bruce and John Stokoe. Society of Antiquaries of Newcastle-upon-Tyne. 130 tunes.

1888   *The Besom Maker*, Heywood Sumner, Longmans Green, London. 9 songs.

1888–1901 *Songs and Ballads of the West*, S. Baring-Gould and H. Fleetwood Sheppard, 4 parts. Methuen, London. 110 songs.

         Songs of the West, a revised edition of the above in one volume under the musical editorship of Cecil Sharp. Methuen, London. 1905. 121 songs.

1891   *Traditional Tunes*, Frank Kidson. Taphouse, Oxford. 109 songs.

1891   *English Folk Songs*, W. A. Barrett. Novello, London. 54 songs.

1893   *English County Songs*, Lucy Broadwood and J. A. Fuller-Maitland. Cramer, London. 95 songs.

1895   *A Garland of County Songs*, S. Baring-Gould and H. Fleetwood Sheppard. Methuen, London. 54 songs.

1899–1931 *Journal of the Folk-Song Society*, 8 vols, 35 parts. London. 1700 tunes and songs (including some Gaelic songs). The Society was amalgamated with the English Folk Dance Society in 1932 and the Journal can now be obtained from the English Folk Dance and Song Society (see next entry).

         Journal of the English Folk Dance and Song Society. London. *In progress.* The Journal can be obtained from the English Folk Dance and Song Society, Cecil Sharp House, Regents Park Road, London N.W.1.

1904   *Wiltshire Folk Songs and Carols*, Geoffrey Hill. W. Mate, Bournemouth. 9 songs.

1908   *English Traditional Songs and Carols*, Lucy Broadwood. Boosey, London. 48 songs.

1908   *Folk Songs from Dorset*,[1] H. E. D. Hammond, Novello, London. 16 songs.

1908   *Folk Songs from the Eastern Countries*,[1] R. Vaughan Williams. Novello, London. 15 songs.

1909   *Folk Songs from Hampshire*,[1] G. B. Gardiner. Novello, London. 16 songs.

1912   *Folk Songs from Sussex*,[1] W. P. Merrick. Novello, London. 15 songs.

1912   *Folk Songs for Schools*, Set 6, R. Vaughan Williams. Novello, London. 11 songs.

1912   *Ships, Sea Songs and Shanties*, W. B. Whall. Jas. Brown, Glasgow. 51 songs.

1913   *Folk Songs from Sussex*, George Butterworth. Augener, London. 11 songs.

1915   *Ten English Folk Songs*, Clive Carey. Curwen, London. 10 songs.

1919   *Eight Traditional Carols*, R. Vaughan Williams. Stainer and Bell, London. 8 songs.

1921   *North Countrie Ballads, Songs and Pipe Tunes*, W. G. Whitaker. Curwen, London. 58 tunes and songs.

1921–26   *The Shanty Book*, R. R. Terry, 2 vols. Curwen, London. 64 songs.

1922   *Folk Songs for Schools*, Set 8, H. E. D. Hammond. Novello, London. 9 songs.

1924   *Six Folk Songs from Norfolk*, E. J. Moeran. Augener, London. 6 songs.

1925   *Last Leaves of Traditional Ballads and Ballad Airs*, Gavin Greig and Alexander Keith. The Buchan Club, Aberdeen. 250 songs. The songs were collected in Aberdeenshire, Scotland, but several are also known in England.

1926   *A Garland of English Folk Songs*, Frank Kidson and Alfred Moffat. Asherberg, Hopwood & Crew, London. 60 songs.

1927   *The Seven Seas Shanty Book*, J. Sampson. Boosey, London. 42 songs.

1927   *A Book of Shanties*, C. Fox Smith. Methuen, London. 31 songs.

1927   *Folk Songs from the North Countrie*, Frank Kidson. Ascherberg, Hopwood and Crew. 60 songs.

1929   *English Peasant Songs*, Frank Kidson, Ethel Kidson and Alfred Moffat. Ascherberg, Hopwood and Crew. 60 songs.

1961   *Shanties from the Seven Seas*, Stanley Hugill. Routledge and Kegan Paul, London, 1961. Not all are English.

A SELECTION OF ANGLO–AMERICAN SONG COLLECTIONS

1929   *British Ballads from Maine*, Phillips Barry, Fannie Eckstorm and Mary Winslow Smith. Yale University Press and Oxford University Press. 85 songs.

1929   *Traditional Ballads of Virginia*, Arthur Kyle Davis. Harvard University Press and Oxford University Press. 148 songs.

1929   *Ballads and Sea Songs from Nova Scotia*, W. Roy Mackenzie. Harvard University Press. 160 songs.

[1] Reprinted in one volume as *English County Folk Songs*, 1961.

1933   *Ballads and Sea Songs of Newfoundland*, Elizabeth Bristol Greenleaf
         and Grace Yarrow Mansfield. Harvard University Press and
         Oxford University Press. 100 songs.
1934   *Folk Songs from Newfoundland*, Maud Karpeles. Oxford University
         Press. 30 songs.
1946   *Ozark Folk Songs*. 4 vols. Vance Randolph. State Historical Research
         Society, Columbia, Missouri. 800 songs.
1950   *Traditional Songs from Nova Scotia*, Helen Creighton and Doreen
         Senior. Ryerson Press, Toronto. 183 songs.
1952–62 *The Frank C. Brown Collection of North Carolina Folklore*. Vol. IV
         (1957) *The Music of the Ballads*. Edited Jan Philip Schinhan. 500
         tunes. (The texts are given in Vol. II, 1952.) Vol. V (1962) *The
         Music of the Folk Songs*. Edited Jan Philip Schinhan. 751 tunes.
         (The texts are given in Vol. III, 1952.)
1960   *More Traditional Ballads of Virginia*, Arthur Kyle Davis. University of
         North Carolina Press and Oxford University Press. 100 songs.
1960–1   *Ancient Ballads Traditionally sung in New England*. 2 vols. Helen
         Hartness Flanders. University of Pennsylvania Press. 130 songs.
1962   *Maritime Folk Songs*, Helen Creighton. Ryerson Press, Toronto. 85
         songs.

The following is an indispensable work of reference. It includes many
unpublished tunes noted by Cecil Sharp.

*The Traditional Tunes of the Child Ballads with their texts according
to the extant records of Great Britain and America.*
Bertrand Harris Bronson, 2 vols. 1959–62. *In progress*. Princeton
University Press.

SONG TEXTS

AS I WALKED THROUGH THE MEADOWS[1]

Now the winter is gone and the summer is come
And the meadows look pleasant and gay;
I met a young damsel, so sweetly sang she,
And her cheeks like the blossoms in May.

I says: Fair maiden, how came you here
In the meadows this morning so soon?
The maid she replied: O I must be excused,
For I'm a-feared you will lead me astray.

Then I took this fair maid by her lily-white hand,
On the green mossy bank we sat down,
And I placèd a kiss on her sweet rosy lips
And the small birds were singing all round.

When we arose from the green mossy bank
To the meadows we wandered away.
I placèd my love on a primrosy bank
And I plucked her a handful of may.

When I returned she gave me a smile
And thanked me for what I had done.
I placèd a sprig on her snowy-white breast,
And, believe me, there's never a thorn.

Then early next morning I made her my bride
That the world should have nothing to say.
The bells they did ring and the bridesmaids did sing[2]
And I crowned her the sweet Queen of May.

Sung by Shepherd Hayden at Bampton, Oxfordshire, September 1909. For another version of the tune, see p. 96.

---

[1] For tune see p. 88.
[2] Usually, 'and the birds they did sing'.

THE SEEDS OF LOVE

I sowed the seeds of love,
'Twas early in the Spring,
In April and May and in June likewise
When small birds they do sing,
When small birds they do sing.

My garden is planted well
With flowers everywhere,
But I had not the liberty to choose for myself
Of the flowers that I loved dear.

My gardener he stood by.
I asked him to choose for me.
He chose me the violet, the lily and the pink,
But these I refused all three.

The violet I forsook
Because it fades so soon.
The lily and the pink I did overlook
And I vowed I'd stay till June.

For in June there is a red rosebud
And that's the flower for me.
So I pulled and I pluckèd at the red rosebud
Till I gainèd the willow tree.

For the willow tree will twist
And the willow tree will twine.
I wish I was in a young man's arms
That once had this heart of mine.

My gardener he stood by
And he told me to take good care;
For in the middle of the red rosebud
There grew a sharp thorn there.

I told him I'd take no care
Until I felt the smart.
I pulled and I pluckèd at the red rosebud
Till it pierced me to my heart.

I locked up my garden gate,
Resolving to keep the key,
But a young man came a-courting me
And he stole my heart away.

My garden is over-run,
No flowers in it grew,
For the beds that were once covered with sweet thyme,
They are now over-run with rue.

Come all you false young men
That leave me here to complain,
For the grass that is now trodden under foot
In time it will rise again.

Sung by Mr Joseph Alcock at Sibford Gower, Oxfordshire, September 1922. A version sung by John England at Hambridge, Somerset, September 1903 (see p. 102), was the first folk song that Cecil Sharp noted. The incident is described in the biography of Cecil Sharp by A. H. Fox Strangways and Maud Karpeles (Oxford University Press, 2nd edition, 1955, p. 33).

HENRY MARTIN

There were three brothers in merry Scotland,
In Scotland there were three,
And they did cast lots which of them should go, should go, should go
And turn robber all on the salt sea.

The lot it fell first upon Henry Martin,
The youngest of all the three;
That he should turn robber all on the salt sea, salt sea, salt sea,
For to maintain his two brothers and he.

He had not been sailing but a long winter's night
And a part of a short winter's day,
Before he espied a stout lofty ship, lofty ship, lofty ship
Come a-bibbing down on him straightway.

Hullo! Hullo! cried Henry Martin,
What makes you sail so nigh?
I'm a rich merchant ship bound for fair London town, London town, London
town.

Will you please for to let me pass by?

O no, O no, cried Henry Martin,
That thing it never could be,
For I am turned robber all on the salt sea, salt sea, salt sea,
For to maintain my two brothers and me.

Come lower your topsail and brail up your mizzen
And bring your ship under my lee,
Or I will give you a full flowing ball, flowing ball, flowing ball,
And your dear bodies drown in the salt sea.

O no, we won't lower our lofty topsail,
Nor bow ourselves under your lee,
And you shan't take from us our rich merchant goods, merchant goods, merchant
goods,
Nor point our bold guns to the sea.

With broadside and broadside and at it they went
For fully two hours or three,
Till Henry Martin gave to her the death shot, the death shot, the death shot,
And straight to the bottom went she.

Bad news, bad news to old England came,
Bad news to fair London town,
There's been a rich vessel and she's cast away, cast away, cast away,
And all of the merry men drowned.

    The tune was noted from Mrs Lucy White at Hambridge, Somerset, April
1905. Mrs White did not remember the words and the present text has been
compiled from other versions.
    Reprinted from *Selected Edition*, Vol. 1, by permission of Messrs Novello & Co.

MY BONNY BOY

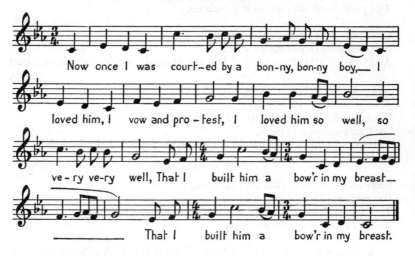

Now once I was court-ed by a bon-ny, bon-ny boy,— I loved him, I vow and pro-test, I loved him so well, so ve-ry ve-ry well, That I built him a bow'r in my breast— That I built him a bow'r in my breast.

Now once I was courted by a bonny, bonny boy.
I loved him, I vow and protest;
I loved him so well, so very, very well,
That I built him a bower in my breast,
That I built him a bower in my breast.

Now up the green valley and down the long alley,
Like one that is troubled in mind,
I called and I did hoot and played upon my lute,
But no bonny, bonny boy could I find.

Now I lookèd east and I lookèd west
Where the sun it shone wonderful warm,
But who should I spy but my bonny, bonny boy,
He was locked in another girl's arms.

Now the girl that does enjoy my bonny, bonny boy,
I'm sure she is never to blame.
For many a long night she has robbed me of my rest,
But she never shall do it again.

Sung by Miss Sarah Smith at Harrison Street, Gray's Inn Road, London, November 1907.
Reprinted from *Selected Edition*, Vol. 1 by permission of Messrs Novello & Co.

BUSHES AND BRIARS

Through bush-es and through bri-ars I late-ly took my way. All for to hear the small birds sing And the lambs to ___ skip and play, ___ All for to hear the small birds sing And the lambs to ___ skip and play

Through bushes and through briars
I lately took my way,
All for to hear the small birds sing
And the lambs to skip and play,
All for to hear the small birds sing
And the lambs to skip and play.

I overheard my own true love,
Her voice it was so clear:
Long time I have been waiting for
The coming of my dear.

Sometimes I am uneasy
And troubled in my mind,
Sometimes I think I'll go to my love
And tell to him my mind.

And if I should go to my love,
My love he will say nay,
If I show to him my boldness
He'll ne'er love me again.

Noted by Ralph Vaughan Williams from Mr Pottipher at Ingrave, Essex, December 1903.

Reprinted from *English County Songs* by permission of Mrs R. Vaughan Williams and Messrs Novello & Co.

THE TREES THEY DO GROW HIGH[1]

The trees they do grow high
And the leaves they do grow green;
The time is gone and past, my love,
That you and I have seen.
It's a cold winter's night, my love,
When you and I must lie alone.
The bonny lad is young, but he's growing.

O father, dear father,
I've feared you've done my harm,
You've married me to a boy
And I fear he is too young.
O daughter, dearest daughter,
And if you stay at home and wait along of me
A lady you shall be while he's growing.

We'll send him to the college
For one year or two,
And then perhaps in time, my love,
A man he may grow.
I will buy you a bunch of white ribbons
To tie about his bonny, bonny waist
To let the ladies know that he's married.

At the age of sixteen,
O he was a married man;
At the age of seventeen
She brought to him a son;
At the age of eighteen, my love,
O his grief was growing grief,
And so she put an end to his growing.[2]

I made my love a shroud
Of the holland so fine;
And every stitch she put in it
The tears came trickling down.
O once I had a sweetheart,
But now I have got never a one,
So fare you well, my own true love, for ever.

[1] The tune with variants is given on p. 33.
[2] The last two lines of this stanza are evidently corrupt. In other versions they usually run
thus:
    O his grave was growing green
    And that soon put an end of his growing.

He is dead and buried
And in the churchyard laid.
The green grass is over him
So very, very thick.
O once I had a sweetheart,
But now I have got never a one.
So fare you well, my own true lover, for ever.

The above is the complete text as sung by Mr Harry Richards at Curry Rivel, Somerset, July 1904.

The text is practically the same as that published by Novello, to whom acknowledgment is made.

HARES ON THE MOUNTAINS[1]

Young women they'll run like hares on the mountains,
Young women they'll run like hares on the mountains.
If I were but a young man, I'd soon go a-hunting.
   To my right fol the diddle dero,
   To my right fol diddle dee.

Young women they'll sing like birds in the bushes,
Young women they'll sing like birds in the bushes.
If I were but a young man, I'd go and bang those bushes.

Young women they'll swim like ducks in the water,
Young women they'll swim like ducks in the water.
If I were but a young man, I'd go and swim after.

Sung by Mrs Louie Hooper and Mrs Lucy White at Hambridge, Somerset, September 1903.

Printed by permission of Messrs Novello & Co.

I'M SEVENTEEN COME SUNDAY

As I walked out one May morning,
One May morning so early,
I overtook a handsome maid
Just as the sun was a-rising.
     With my rue dum a day,
     Fol the diddle i day,
     Fol the dol the diddle i day.

[1] For the tune, see p. 81.

Her shoes were bright and her stockings white
And her buckles shone like silver.
She had a black and a rolling eye
And her hair hung over her shoulder.

How old are you, my fair pretty maid?
How old are you, my honey?
She answered me quite cheerfully:
I am seventeen come Sunday.

Will you marry me, my fair pretty maid?
Will you marry me, my honey?
She answered me quite cheerfully:
I dare not for my mammy.

If you'll come unto my mammy's house
When the moon is shining brightly
I will come down and let you in
And my mammy shall not hear me.

I went unto her mammy's house
When the moon was shining brightly.
She did come down and let me in,
And I laid in her arms till morning.

Now soldier, will you marry me?
Now is your time or never.
For if you do not marry me,
I am undone for ever.

And now she is the soldier's wife
And the soldier loves her dearly.
The drum and fife is her [or my] delight,
And a merry old man is mine O.

Sung by Mr William Spearing at Ile Brewers, Somerset, April 1904. His tune is given on p. 82. A better tune was sung by Mrs Lucy White at Hambridge, Somerset, July 1904 (see p. 86). Mrs White remembered only a couple of stanzas, but the words printed above will fit her tune, except for the refrain, which in her version was:

> With my rue dum day,
> Fol the diddle dol,
> Fol the dol the diddle dum the day.

A close version of this text is used in the publications of Messrs Novello, to whom acknowledgment is made.

INDEX